PATRIOTIC REBEL

John C. Calhoun

Born: March 18, 1782
Died: March 31, 1850

Hailed as a champion of liberty, attacked as a supporter of slavery, John C. Calhoun was one of the most controversial figures in a stormy era of United States political history. As Representative, Senator, Secretary of State and Vice President, he struggled to reconcile the interests of his beloved Southland with the needs of the Federal government during the decades that saw the nation move toward civil war. This is the tragic story of a man whose greatness and leadership helped draw the South toward the disaster he so desperately dreaded and tried to avoid.

Patriotic Rebel
John C. Calhoun

∽ **by** ∽
WILLIAM D. CRANE

JULIAN MESSNER Ⓜ NEW YORK

Published by Julian Messner
a division of Simon & Schuster, Inc.
1 West 39th Street, New York, N.Y. 10018
All Rights Reserved

To Peg Crane

Printed in the United States of America

ISBN 0-671-32494-2 Cloth Trade
     0-671-32497-7 MCE

Library of Congress Catalog Card No. 72-176377

ACKNOWLEDGEMENTS

My thanks are due to the many friends who have aided in the production of this book, and especially to W. Edwin Hemphill, editor of "Papers of John C. Calhoun"; Frederick R. Goff, Chief of Rare Book Division, and Roy P. Basler, Chief of Reference Department, manuscript division, Library of Congress; Mrs. Barbara H. Littlefield, Abbeville County Development Board; Judith A. Schiff, Chief Reference Specialist, Yale University Library; and Mrs. Priscilla H. Sutcliffe, Special Collection Department, Clemson University.

W. D. Crane

"My end is probably near—perhaps very near. Before I reach it I have but one serious thought to gratify. It is to see my country quieted under some arrangement (alas, I know not what!) that will be satisfactory to all, and safe to the South."

John C. Calhoun

"He was a man of undoubted genius and of commanding talent. All the country and all the world admit that. His mind was both perceptive and vigorous. It was clear, quiet and strong."

Daniel Webster

∽ I ∽

The date was March 18, 1782. The place was eight miles south of the town of Abbeville, in the northwestern corner of South Carolina in the foothills of the Appalachian mountains. It was an area of small farms peopled by pioneers. The day was rainy and bleak, and a blustering wind swayed the tall pines and cedars, tore at the grape and pawpaw vines on the surrounding hillsides and made the tall canes rattle in the swamps.

In a two-story frame house, the only one of like construction for miles around, a little boy opened his eyes for the first time on a world that was to be his for the next sixty-eight years. His name was John Caldwell Calhoun. He had two brothers, William and James, a sister, Catherine, and his mother and father, Martha and Patrick, whose family had come over from Ireland forty-nine years before. Patrick himself had started the settlement on February 18, 1752, and called the district "Long Cane."

All that little John saw at first glance was a series of faces, some white and some black, gazing down at him and making strange sounds, a crackling fire on the hearth and curious objects hanging from the ceiling. This was all peaceful enough, but the world around him was actually in a state of crisis. For seven years, the American colonists had been battling to break away from England, their mother country, and South Carolina had borne a very large part of the hardships of war. In 1780, the British Colonel Tarleton had ridden through the state, laying waste the countryside on his way to assist at the capture of the capital city of Charleston. The whole state suffered agony, and soon there were no American troops left in South Carolina. Ravaging bands of armed men scoured the state, murdering in cold blood, confiscating estates and burning houses of patriots. Horace Walpole in England declared: "We look on America as at our feet."

Then an unbelievably daring march by General George Washington from the Hudson River to Virginia with 2,000 continental troops and 4,000 French turned the tide. At four o'clock on the afternoon of October 7, 1781, Colonel O'Hara, acting for Lord Cornwallis, who was confined to his tent, gave up his sword to General Washington as a token of surrender. Five months later, the little boy in the uplands of South Carolina opened his eyes during the birth of a new country in which he was destined to play a vital role.

As soon as he was able to understand, what he heard

was not a series of stories from some fairy-tale book. He heard about the Revolution, of course, but what was even more terrifying were the tales of Indian warfare. They were fresh in the mind of his father, who had played a very personal part in them, and he enjoyed reminiscing to all who would listen. The Cherokee (upland) Indians, one of the most advanced tribes of the period, held a vast territory to the west of Virginia and North and South Carolina. They had been peaceful until 1760, when, because of the slaughter of several members of the tribe after the fall of Fort Duquesne, they turned on the settlers of South Carolina in all their fury, driving them from their homes or scalping them mercilessly. In one ambush, John's grandmother and an uncle were brutally butchered, many others killed and children carried into captivity. Patrick Calhoun kept his old bullet-punctured hat hanging by the fireplace, perhaps as a hint to any visitors that gruesome stories lay behind it.

The talk that John heard during his early years was not all about the Revolution or even Indian fighting. There was much discussion of politics, a very vital subject to the new nation that had just freed itself from an oppressive rule. The people of the Long Cane country were quite isolated and felt very deeply the need for representation in any government that might develop, and in the Calhoun kitchen there was much arguing as to what this government should and should not be. John's father was the natural leader in these talks. It is reported that once, in colonial times, he had brought an armed body of settlers to the voting place at Charleston and voted himself and two friends into the Assembly. John, as he grew older, liked to sit and listen to these talks. He had great love and respect for his father and paid special attention to his remarks.

Walking several miles to a crude log house school in all kinds of weather and doing chores in and out of the house constituted his life for his first twelve years. At school, he learned to read and write and do simple sums, and the chores on a working plantation taught him a sense of responsibility that never left him. He enjoyed the life. He loved the outdoors and, on his way to school, reveled in the smell of the pines and the taste of the wild strawberries and juicy pawpaws, and he had fun stirring the possums and otters from the thick underbrush.

Then Moses Waddel entered his life. Mr. Waddel was an itinerant preacher who visited the Calhouns in 1794 as an applicant for the position of the local Presbyterian minister. He held the post for some time—how successfully is not recorded. Two things about his first meeting with the Calhouns, however, are sure. Sitting around the fire with the family, he noticed a youthful head with very disheveled hair and strong features that peeked at him around the kitchen door and was quickly withdrawn, and he was also much struck with John's sister, Catherine. Later, he started the disheveled-headed boy on his real education, and within a year he married Catherine Calhoun. The Waddels then opened a school at Willington not far from the Calhoun plantation, and John was promptly enrolled. Mr. Waddel was considered to be an excellent teacher. The curriculum was heavy and the hours extremely long, but John was used to working early and late and was doing very well when tragedy struck the Waddels. Before a year was past, Catherine died. Distraught with grief, Moses Waddel closed the school and took up again the work of an itinerant preacher.

John was left alone, but this was not an unusual situation for him. His brothers had gone away to work some time before, and he had been left much to his own devices. In this case, though, there was a factor that made loneliness more than bearable. Mr. Waddel had accumulated a small library and, left to himself, John took full advantage of it. He had learned to enjoy reading, and he looked carefully over the titles. There was *Ancient History,* by Rollins; Cooke's *Voyages; Essay on Human Understanding,* by John Locke; and William Robertson's *History of Charles II.*

This last was in four thick volumes. Undismayed, John picked up the first and glanced at the opening pages. In discussing the domination of the Roman Empire in the early centuries, Robertson spoke of the severe rule inflicted on other nations and the high taxes imposed. At one point, he wrote, "The vanquished people resumed their arms with fresh spirit—animated by the love of liberty." John's thoughts went back to his father's oft-repeated statement that "the best government is one in which the individual has the most liberty." John read most of the four volumes and turned to other books. He became so enthralled by what he read that he scarcely left the house. In John Locke's *Essay on Human Understanding*, he was much impressed by the emphasis on a true understanding without prejudice, and vowed to himself that he would try to follow this advice.

Six weeks went by. They didn't seem long to John because he was enjoying himself in his new-found world of books, but the lack of exercise and fresh air was gradually telling on his general health. When Moses Waddel came back from his travels, he found John in a very weak state. In fact, he was so alarmed that he wrote Mrs. Calhoun that he thought the boy should be taken home and properly cared for. John's mother responded at once and soon John was back in the Long Canes country.

Home was an ideal place to recover his health, but once he had his strength back, its loneliness faced him with a challenge. His father had died early in 1796 while John was at Mr. Waddel's, just a few weeks before his sister. His two brothers, William and James, were away working in distant cities, so his mother and his young brother, Patrick, were his only companions at home. There were no outside playmates. He loved his mother, who was always a great source of strength, but he particularly missed his father, the old Indian fighter, with his stern Calvinistic code of morals and his unremitting belief in the rights of the individual. He missed listening to the political discussions around the hearth and the talks alone with his father. Whatever the subject, old Patrick was sure to lead the conversation around to his favorite contention that everything an individual did should be motivated by certain inalienable rights which nature and reason seemed to establish. This was repeated so often that John came to believe it with all the sincerity of his belief in God and the Bible, acquired from his mother.

Patrick had left John and his mother a fairly large tract of land and some thirty-five Negro slaves. This meant work, and John soon found that work can replace loneliness. Fortunately, he enjoyed working and soon settled down to the routine of plantation life. Up before sunrise, feeding, milking, breeding cattle, plowing, sowing, reaping and a myriad of minor tasks constituted the long day. To be sure, he had his slaves to help him, but he was most just and kind and never wanted to overburden them. He often joined them in the fields even in the blistering Southern sun. He was especially fond of one young Negro named Sawney whose father, Abram, had been one of Patrick Calhoun's first slaves. Sawney and he would plant cotton together, John plowing the furrows and Sawney following, dropping in the precious seeds. After this preliminary work, John took special, personal interest in the cultivation of the cotton field. It was a vital part of the plantation's success, and he could not be careless. Grass and weeds must be kept out, and there was a constant battle with aphids and corn-field ants. To John, the rich reward came with the opening of the unspotted white flower of the upland cotton and then, when the leaves fell off, with the precious ball of cotton itself.

John grew to love the life of a planter, and he made up his mind that this was to be his life's work. He was always happy to be out in the open, and the challenge of growing things and meeting the hazards of nature continually inspired him. Also, although his mother was a very clever woman and John depended a great deal on her common sense and shrewdness, he knew that she could not bear the physical burdens alone, and that he must stay with her. So, for the time being, reading and the study of books had to be put aside. There were very few books, and there was very little time to read had there been more. The few spare moments in a day gave John a chance for the hunting and fishing which he loved. Fishing, especially, lured him as it gave him time to think over the ideas he had gleaned from Mr. Waddel's library. Sawney usually went with him and made a good listener when John put his thoughts into words.

John also spent much time talking with his mother. She was an ardent Presbyterian, and John acquired the religious instinct which remained with him all his life more from example than precept. She was very friendly with many of the South Carolina Huguenots, who had an inborn courtliness and a certain aristocratic sensitivity. This graciousness of manner brushed off on her, and she passed it on to her son. John was most receptive to it, and it became a permanent part of his nature. Their talks together had, of course, much to do with the management of the plantation and its many difficult problems, but his mother was a most intelligent listener and the theories of

John Locke and William Robertson, still fresh in John's mind, had their full share of analysis.

Newspapers were a rare commodity in the Piedmont area. There was no post office in Abbeville, and it took a full two weeks in good weather for a wagon to reach there from Charleston, so for long periods the upland people were quite in the dark as to the progress and problems of the new nation. One day, John came across a paper left behind by some wanderer in the area. It was a copy of the South Carolina *Gazette* dated April, 1798. After work and late into the night by tallow candle, he eagerly read every word, carefully penciling passages of particular interest for discussion with his mother. One, especially, he marked heavily, for it disturbed him. It was from a speech delivered during the Fifth Session of Congress, and read in part: "The negotiations with the French Republic are at an end, and there is no chance of an accommodation taking place between the two countries. . . ." In the solitude of the backwoods, he had not heard of the strange doings of citizen Genet, Ambassador from the new French Republic who was fitting out privateers in United States ports, declaring war on England and antagonizing not only the Tory element in America but to a large extent even the patriots. To John, the passage was incomprehensible. His father had often told him of Lafayette and Rochambeau, and of how 4,000 French soldiers marched side by side with the colonial troops for the first time during Washington's famous march from the Hudson River to Virginia to help in the defeat of Lord

Cornwallis. Why then, he wondered, was there any disagreement? And yet, the *Gazette* further reported Congressional discussions of raising a militia and of strength-
ening the defenses of New York Harbor and other
strategic points in the nation, and printed a speech by
President John Adams, who had succeeded President
Washington the year before. Among other things, Adams
said, "I will never send another minister to France without assurance that he will be received, respected and
honored as the representative of a great, free, powerful
and independent nation. . . ." While confusing to John,
all this stirred in him a strong desire to know more about
the politics of the new United States.

Fate is no respecter of logic, and often the most trivial
happenings will bring far from trivial results. In the summer of 1800, John's brother James came home for a short
visit. He was working as a clerk in Charleston and was on
a short vacation, and he was delighted to see his younger
brother. They had been quite close during their early
years, and he and John had long talks. Much of this was
reminiscing and laughing over the vast difference between the city life of Charleston and that of the forest-
clad Piedmont area. When the conversation turned to
more serious matters, James was struck by the ease with
which his brother talked and the grasp he appeared to
have on almost all matters. James's own education had
been limited, and he was so impressed that one day he
suggested to John that he should take up the profession
of law. He was met by a shrug of the shoulders and the

assurance that such a move was impossible. John said he loved the life of a planter and fully intended to continue at it.

James was almost as stubborn as his brother, and he decided to take the matter up with his mother. She was, however, equally adamant. She needed John on the plantation. She could not carry the burden of it alone and, besides, John was most enthusiastic about a planter's life.

This might have ended the matter and changed the course of history except that John himself was doing a little more thinking. For several nights he lay awake musing over the prospect of a professional life. His brother was being most persistent, and the reading of the *Gazette* had turned his thoughts to the doings of the outside world. Why wouldn't such a move be a good way to keep in touch with the problems of the new nation? Finally, he reached a decision. He told James that on two conditions he would consider studying for the law: His mother had to give her consent, and sufficient money would have to somehow be raised for at least seven years of schooling. This last condition, he told James, was because only a thorough education would suffice. He didn't want anything that was merely second best.

This was a poser, but James worked on his mother and finally persuaded her that John's natural aptitude for study and his skill in expressing his ideas were lost behind the plow. So it was decided. John would have more schooling and then study for the law. Mr. Waddel had remarried and reopened his school. There was more emphasis on Latin and the classics so necessary in college. Two years should prepare John for any college, and this choice was left up to him. Harvard was the oldest college in the colonies, but John had often been told that Yale was popular among the aristocratic youth on the coast as their first choice after Oxford or Cambridge, depending on the degree of Toryism maintained by their parents. It was called, by them, the "Athens of America." John chose Yale.

John spent the next two years in intensive study. He was nineteen years old, full of ambition and determined to carry out the agreement made with his mother and brother. The Waddel school, or "Academy" as it was called, was lodged in log cabins, the course of study was rigid and the hours long. The early rising didn't disturb John. It was merely a continuation of his normal schedule, sunrise to eight or nine o'clock at night, studying by torch or candlelight. The teachers were not unlike his father—stern and uncompromising, with the Scotch Presbyterian blood of their forebears flowing through their veins.

The emphasis was on the classics. Elementary Latin grammar led to the reading of the satires of Horace and the beautifully worded poetry of Ovid. It was not at all unusual to be assigned five hundred to a thousand lines of Virgil for memorizing. In all this, John found much that could be related to the government and morality of his own time and it gave him much food for thought. The conditions for study were far from being the best.

Much of the work was done outside under the trees sitting on hard chairs, but Mr. Waddel and his staff were excellent teachers. By 1802, John was ready to present himself for enrollment in the junior class at Yale.

Tragedy marred his last year, for his mother died in 1801. He had visited her only a few days before her death and received the news back at Mr. Waddel's. The loss was a bitter one, but he kept at his studies with even more of his usual conscientiousness. He felt very deeply his indebtedness to her for any success he might achieve.

~ II ~

In the fall of 1802, the packet boat from Charleston deposited lanky John Calhoun in New Haven with a bag of clothes and money in his pocket for tuition. He had never before been so far away from home and was still somewhat dazzled by what he had seen as he passed through Charleston on his way to the docks. He couldn't forget the rows of brick Georgian houses, with their iron grills, tiered piazzas and general air of elegance, or the lofty spire of St. Michael's Church pointing its many-tiered finger to heaven as guardian of the morals of gay Charlestonians. Compared to this, New Haven was a village, although had he not seen Charleston, it would have seemed a city to the young man from the back country. The streets were sandy, with few houses, many of them built in the Charleston style. Cows grazed undisturbed on the green by Yale College.

John had certain fears quite natural to a boy with only a log cabin education, however excellent his teachers.

He knew there would be young men fresh from Exeter and Andover preparatory schools. Also, the dearth of newspapers in the Long Canes left him somewhat confused as to what was going on in the outside world, and he felt that his classmates would look on him as an ignorant boor. Besides, he was concerned because Yale was predominantly Federalist. Its president, the Reverend Timothy Dwight, grandson of Jonathan Edwards, despised Republicanism and fought against it with all of his Calvinistic vigor. It was a question in John's mind whether or not the Reverend Dwight would tolerate him, but he was determined to defend his beliefs even against the powerful logic of "Pope" Dwight (as he was known behind his back), no matter what the results might be.

In Connecticut Hall, a four-story brick building, he paid the necessary fees: four dollars for the first-quarter tuition, fifty cents for his room in Connecticut Hall, sixty cents for repairs and other charges and thirty-three cents for sweeping and making beds. With the receipt in his pocket, he became a member of the class of 1804. No examination was required. He was then shown the book of laws, a most Puritanical list of what students should not do, which he dutifully signed. He found that he must not deny the Holy Scriptures, speak blasphemously or be guilty of robbery, forgery or dueling, on pain of fine or dismissal. The fourth law he found rather difficult to believe. It read: "If any Scholar shall assault, wound or strike the President, a Professor or a Tutor, or shall maliciously or designedly break their windows or doors, he

shall be expelled." Then he went through a curious for-
mality. At Yale there were two literary societies: the
Linnonians and the Brothers in Unity. Membership was
entirely a matter of chance, the students being assigned
to one or the other alternately in alphabetical order. John
duly signed the rolls of the Linnonians. Actually, he had
no particular desire to join any society. Had he had any
foreknowledge of the two groups, he would have se-
lected the Brothers in Unity, to which most Southern
men belonged.

John was assigned to a room which he shared with
another student. It was comfortable enough, and even
had a fireplace; but it was not too far from the local prison
and insane asylum, and the sounds from them were at
times both disturbing and terrifying. John had bought a
newspaper, and the first thing he did was to clear up a
little of his ignorance of world affairs. The news columns
were full of the exploits of Napoleon Bonapart, who was
creating a crisis in Europe which threatened to implicate
the new United States.

The news was, of course, some two or three weeks late,
but as the days went by and John made a few friends, he
was able to fill in the gaps. Politics and international relations were the chief topics among the more serious students, and Thomas Jefferson, the newly elected president,
came in for criticism among the strongly Federalist New
Englanders. As the choice of the Republicans and a
Southerner, the new president was, to John, the hero of
the day. This tall, not very handsome Virginian was a

man after his own heart, a man who seemed to voice the sentiments not only of Tom Paine in his *Rights of Man* but of old Patrick Calhoun, who had persistently insisted upon the rights of the individual in any government. New England Federalists were getting desperate and John not only had to listen to criticism of Republicans from most of his classmates but also had to read in the papers what was said by many public figures. Senator Pickering of Massachusetts, after remarking that democracy was merely another name for atheism and terror, added: "The principles of our Revolution point to the remedy—separation." John had great faith in the new Union, and he prayed that Jefferson would find a way to reconcile the New Englanders to the new regime.

He was gaining confidence in himself as the weeks went by, and his original fear of competing with Northern school graduates was fast dissipating as he talked and debated with them. The same thing was true in the classroom. He found that he could not only keep up with his classmates but in many ways surpass them. He had a rather surprising proof of this in his senior year in a class conducted by President Dwight. The ardent Federalist was holding forth on politics, using as his text *Principles of Moral & Political Philosophy*, by William Paley, an English theologian. It was a statement of the theory of utilitarianism, an eighteenth-century code that held that the greatest good of the greatest number is the goal of political morality. Dr. Dwight suddenly turned to John and asked what he thought was the legitimate source of power. John had been brought up in a minority group, his father had forced certain concessions from the Charleston majority and his views were quite opposite to Paley's. He faced up fearlessly to the Doctor and talked at great length with a logic that surprised even himself. The discussion lasted for an hour and, though probably not convinced, Doctor Dwight was so impressed that he said afterwards that "the young man has talent enough to be President of the United States."

John had been elected to Phi Beta Kappa, an honor fraternity founded at the time of the Revolution at William and Mary College. At their meetings, he had often debated such subjects as "Is government founded on the social compact?" After the discussion with Doctor Dwight on the majority in government, he began to do some significant thinking. He had agreed with his mother that he would study law, and that was the basis on which he was enrolled at Yale. He never had been enthusiastic about the profession. It seemed to him that a lawyer, since he was called upon to defend the guilty as well as the innocent, was blurring the difference between good and evil. It was a dilemma. Politics as a lifework was becoming more and more attractive. Doctor Dwight's casual prediction that he might become President of the United States, although he didn't take it seriously, did not lessen the attractiveness of government work. It was not in his nature, however, to go back on an agreement, especially with his mother, and he pushed the idea aside.

Then commencement exercises loomed on the horizon.

He learned that he was to graduate with honors, and he looked forward to the day with justifiable pride. He was to deliver an English oration and, rather significantly, the subject chosen was "The Qualifications Necessary to Form a Statesman." He had worked long and conscientiously on it when he was struck by a high fever and was confined to bed. This, in itself, was a bitter blow. Although the natural thing would have been to convalesce at home, in his condition, the prospect of the arduous trip to South Carolina seemed out of the question. Besides, he had arranged to go to Litchfield to attend the law school conducted by Tappan Reeves. He was faced with the dreary prospect of staying in the deserted college until the following fall with few friends and little money.

In Charleston, however, was a widow by the name of Floride Bonneau Colhoun, who, although maintaining a spelling slightly different from that of the upland Calhouns, was a second cousin. She had heard from John's brother James that her relative was at Yale, and she became interested as Yale was the alma mater of aristocracy. She wrote him a letter inviting him to visit her at her summer place in Newport after graduation, to which he replied hopefully.

To Mrs. Floride Colhoun, Newport, R. I.
New Haven, August 29, 1804

Dear Madam, Yesterday your friendly favor of the 23rd inst. came to hand. Mr. Noble did suggest to

me sometime since, that you expected to spend the
summer in Rhode Island and that you would be glad
to see me there, but did not mention at what place.
Under this uncertainty, it was impossible for me to
act until further information from you. This, however, as I before stated reached me not only late,
but found me ill.

I thank you, Madam, for your kind solicitude re-
garding the present state of my health. I am happy
to assure you that I feel myself making some ad-
vance towards a recovery.

I flatter myself that I shall so far have regained
my health by Commencement that I shall be able to
realize the enjoyment of that Day. But above all,
Madam, I am anxious to recover in order that I may
visit Newport immeditely after Commencement.
Until which time and forever, believe me, dear
Madam, to be with great respect.

                              Yours,
                              John C. Calhoun.

Unfortunately, he did not recover in time for commencement, but Mrs. Colhoun was quite equal to the occasion. It seemed more than natural to offer a sick relative a home and care until his complete recovery. Almost
before he knew it, John was enjoying the hospitality and
loving care of Floride Bonneau Colhoun.

Newport, Rhode Island, had for fifty years been the

mecca for fashionable Carolinians, driven from the coastal
towns by the malaria mosquito. In fact, it had achieved
the title of the "Carolina Hospital." It was an old town,
founded in 1639, and had gone through many vicissi-
tudes, including its destruction by fire by the British.
John was always interested in new places, and he was
fascinated by the few landmarks left. There was the Old
Stone Mill, said to have been a grist mill owned by Bene-
dict Arnold, the Old Brick Market and the Sabbaterian
Church, the oldest in the country.

Aside from these historic sites, Newport was interesting to John as his first intimate contact with aristocracy. September and October went by altogether too
rapidly in the luxury of the Colhoun mansion. It rather
astonished him at first that a distant cousin whom he had
never before met should lavish the care on him that he
received from his hostess. Of course, there was a possible
explanation which didn't occur to John. He was tall and
handsome, a Yale graduate and honor student, and Mrs.
Colhoun had a young daughter, Floride, aged thirteen.
The fact that he was from the back country made little
difference, for Mrs. Colhoun herself had married John
Erving Colhoun, who could hardly claim particularly
aristocratic ancestors. John grew most genuinely fond of
his benefactress. Her graciousness of manner, seemingly
a trait of Huguenots, reminded him of his mother.

John recovered his health and was ready to carry out
his plan of studying law in Abbeville under a certain
George Bowie, a distinguished lawyer who was practic-

ing there. Mrs. Colhoun was preparing to go back to Charleston, and it was arranged that they should all make the trip by packet. After a voyage of twelve days, they reached Charleston and John, much refreshed by his stay at Newport and the sail down the coast, left by stage for Abbeville.

After studying under George Bowie for the balance of the winter months, he was prepared to carry out the plan he had decided on for his future. He would spend a year at the Litchfield, Connecticut, Law School, run by Judge Tappan Reeves and George Gould. It was one of the first law schools in the country with instruction given almost entirely by lectures. John had decided on this for two reasons. Many of his friends, including his roommate, planned to attend, and he had found the New England air most stimulating. The fact that he would be near Newport had a vague corroborative influence on his decision. He had been corresponding quite regularly with Mrs. Colhoun, and she told him she would be driving up to Newport and would be delighted to have him join her and the children in her coach. John accepted with pleasure, met her in Charleston and drove north to Newport. It was a new experience for John, who was accustomed to the public stage or the back of a horse. The coach was a handsome affair drawn by four horses and driven by a gaily livried coachman.

After a short stay in Newport, John took the stage for Litchfield. The law school was housed in a white one-room clapboard and shingle house on the corner of West and Spencer streets. It was simple, but the two men who ran it were far from that. Judge Reeves was judge of the Superior Court of Connecticut, and Mr. Gould, though younger, was an experienced lawyer. There were several classmates from Yale in the group, but John kept much to himself. He concentrated on his studies because that was his nature, but there was another reason why he kept out of town affairs and avoided mixing with the people of Litchfield. It was, he soon found out, a Federalist stronghold. The feeling against President Jefferson was running high, and the talk of a break-up of the Union was heard on all sides. In fact, Judge Reeves and Mr. Gould were ardent separationists. John longed for an opportunity to argue the case, but he realized that as an unknown law student, he would find it futile. This frustration in the field of politics made him more eager than ever to finish the study of law as soon as possible. In one letter to Mrs. Colhoun, he wrote: "I find myself much absorbed by the pursuit of legal knowledge. . . . I find that I must devote almost the whole of my time to that pursuit. . . ." In a letter to a friend, in speaking of the study of law, he wrote: "I can never consider it but a task which my situation forces on me."

In spite of the difficulties of political prejudice and a dislike of the law, John received a diploma on July 29, 1806, with the notation that "he has applied himself to no other regular business and has attended diligently and faithfully to the study of the law." So conscientious was he that, even after receiving his diploma, he stayed on a

few weeks for some additional lectures. Then, by stage
and horseback, he went to Charleston and spent some
time in the law office of a friend. In 1807, he returned to
Abbeville, where he planned to practice among his up-
country friends. His sincerity and skill soon won him a
local reputation, and he was making a success of law in
spite of his dislike of it when an incident occurred that
changed the whole course of his life.

Norfolk, Virginia, which had probably the finest harbor and shipping facilities of any place in the world, was
almost totally destroyed by the British during the Revolution, but by 1807 it was back in business. A British
squadron was lying off the capes to prevent the escape of
some French frigates moored up the bay. American business, however, was going on as usual in June, 1807. On
the 22nd of that month, Commodore Barron took his ship
Chesapeake out of Norfolk Roads under full sail, proudly
flying his official pennant. He was bound with a cargo for
the Mediterranean. It was a beautiful spring day, and he
anticipated no serious happenings as the trip was purely
routine. He had just passed the ten-mile limit when a
British ship, *The Leopard,* came alongside and hailed the
commodore with the word "dispatches." The mutual
carrying of mail was a common custom, and Barron in-
vited their captain on board. No sooner had the *Leopard's* officer stepped on the deck than he demanded that
four sailors who, he claimed, were British deserters be
turned over to him. Commodore Barron quite properly
said that he would not hear of it unless the captain of the

ship from which they had deserted should ask for them. After some argument, the British captain returned to his ship and Barron got under way. No sooner had he gained some speed than the *Leopard* fired a broadside. Barron was on a peaceful mission and was quite unprepared for a sea battle. Before he could get even one gun in position, his ship was so badly damaged that he was forced to give in. Four seamen were taken off, and the *Chesapeake* limped back to Norfolk with its tragic story. Bad news travels fast, and it was not long before the country knew of the insult to the United States. Reaction in the town of Abbeville was no exception. As soon as the news was heard, a committee was formed to write to Washington urging that serious steps be taken.

Quite naturally the young, successful Abbeville lawyer was asked to be on the committee and, furthermore, he was appointed to draft the wording of the protest, which would be read to the townspeople before being sent to Congress. What was more natural than that the popular young lawyer should read it? John was a little fearful, though much flattered. At last he was to have a hand in politics—a small man from a small town, but a voice from the people in true Jeffersonian style. The day for the reading came, the little courthouse was crowded and the committee was on the platform. Standing on the edge was John C. Calhoun, six feet two inches tall with a look of the deepest sincerity on his face, about to make his maiden political speech. He spoke easily, something he had learned in his Phi Beta Kappa debates at Yale. These

debates had been interesting, but purely theoretical. Here
was a question concerning national pride and even the
possibility of war. He reminded his hearers of the Revolution that freed them from the tyranny of England. He
admitted that many of the older men in the room had
been through it and hardly needed reminding, but a new
generation was growing up that perhaps needed to be
told what the Revolution meant. He spoke of Washington's urging that we keep out of foreign entanglements.
He quoted the great patriots of that time, Patrick Henry,
John Adams, Ben Franklin and, last but not least, his
idol, Thomas Jefferson, who was at that time Ambassador
to France. He stressed that the ideals envisioned by all
these men were too precious to be flouted by the British.
He did not urge immediate war, for he knew that the
United States was not prepared for it. He offered a series
of resolutions expressing the sentiments of his community, a copy of which was to be transmitted to the President of the United States. The first two were vital:

> Resolved 1st. that this Assembly view with the
> deepest abhorrence, the unjust and murderous con-
> duct of the British armed vessel *Leopard* to the
> United States frigate *Chesapeake*.
> Resolved 2nd. that it will regard as enemies of our
> country all (should any be so base) who either di-
> rectly or indirectly by action, words or any means
> whatsoever, pretend to justify the said detestable
> conduct of the British.

The speech was roundly applauded and a copy of the resolutions sent to Congress. That might have been the end of it for John. Word got around, however, that a young lawyer in the upland country was wasting his time, and in October of that year he was unanimously elected to the South Carolina Legislature.

A seat in the local House of Representatives! John was elated. A vague thought was coming true. It amused him to recollect how his father had won his seat in the same body at the point of a gun and had held it for thirty years. He wished the old man might have been present when his son won the same distinction following a maiden public address. He was in politics, something he had often dreamed about. While the law business was too profitable to give up at once, and there were certain cases pending that he could not in good conscience neglect, he decided that to have a voice in the government of the Union would be his life's work. C785216 ₥. SCHOOLS

When the Legislature met in the following January, John found he had a chance to defend one of his favorite theories, dating back not only to his father, but to John Locke and Tom Paine. The particular issue concerned the relation between the uplanders and the lowlanders. With the boundaries to the west becoming more flexible, the farming population increased with them, and the new settlers had begun to feel that they were not properly represented in the state. A bill was coming up to adjust this by giving the Charleston majority a final say in the Senate while the upland people would control the House of Representatives. This, to John, was a clear case of the fundamental rights of man. He spoke most convincingly on the subject, and the bill was passed.

At about this time, Republican members of the Legislature were drawing up a slate of nominees for the presidency of the United States to succeed Thomas Jefferson. James Madison was nominated for President, and the names of George Clinton and deWitt Clinton, his nephew, were proposed for the Vice Presidency. As a very recently elected member of the House, Calhoun felt a natural hesitancy about speaking out on such an important occasion. However, the impulse to speak out on anything he thoroughly believed was too strong. Both Clintons were, he told the session, excellent men, but their views on what should be done in the present European crisis were not fully in accord with other members of the Republican Party, and their election might disrupt the party's unanimity. He said that, as he saw it, war with England was inevitable and the country must be run by men dedicated to preparing the United States for an armed conflict. He proposed the name of John Langdon of New Hampshire, a Federalist. His confidence in himself was strengthened when Langdon was nominated, even though he was not later elected.

He was having success in politics, but there was another and much more personal matter in which he was hoping for equal success. He had seen Floride Colhoun constantly on his frequent visits to Newport and had told her mother something of his feelings. He had hesitated to speak to Floride herself, who in 1809 was only fifteen, but in his own heart he felt she was the one girl he wanted to marry.

In 1810, much to his surprise, John found that rumors of his attachment to his cousin were floating around Abbeville. On June 25, he told Mrs. Colhoun about it, adding: "In fact, to me it is quite unaccountable how such an impression should become so universal." Such is the blindness of love. Finally, towards the end of 1810, he broke down and admitted his plans to his friends and wrote to Floride in September.

> I rejoice, my dearest Floride, that the period is fast approaching when it will be no longer necessary to address you through the cold medium of a letter. . . . I am much involved in business at present . . . and in a week, the election for Congress will take place. My opponent is General Elmore of Lawrence, but it is thought that I will succeed by a large majority. . . . Write me before you leave Newport. . . . May God preserve you. Adieu my love; my heart's delight.
>
> I am your true lover
> John C. Calhoun.

On January 8, 1811, he and Floride were married in a thoroughly aristocratic wedding at the Bonneau plantation outside Charleston. Floride Colhoun was seventeen, and John C. Calhoun was twenty-seven.

Graceful, dark-haired Floride was, of course, admired by all, but her tall, handsome husband came in for an unusually careful scrutiny by the fashionably dressed beaux of Charleston society. After all, he was the son of Patrick Calhoun, an upland farmer endowed only with a stern Calvinistic outlook on life, hard working and relentless in opinions, which had never been favorable towards the gay, carefree life of Charleston. Would this young man be able to bridge the gap between the two worlds? Calhoun, of course, was fully aware of every glance in his direction, but it didn't disturb him in the slightest. He had had a taste of both worlds, and he was confident that, with Floride's help, the gap could easily be closed.

They were very much in love and looked forward to life together on their plantation at Bath, on the Savannah River, not far from his brother James. The house was a simple one, a far cry from the luxury of Charleston, but Floride took great pleasure in rearranging rooms and planning decorations. She was very proud of John's success in politics and his general popularity, although she had no particular interest in public affairs. Her Charleston life had never been slanted in that direction, the emphasis in the Colhoun household having been almost entirely on social life and home care. John encouraged her in her activities about the house and garden, smilingly acquiescing in all the changes she carried out, rather relieved to hear little talk of politics. He had not lost his love of plantation life, and he found himself living a sort of double existence—farmer and politician.

Two months before he and Floride were married, he had been almost unanimously elected to the National House of Representatives. This was an honor, but it meant that during most of the winter months, he would have to be away from Floride. To move to Washington would be expensive, and Calhoun had firmly made up his mind that he would be personally responsible for all necessary outlays of money. In fact, he had refused any share of Floride's dowry. Furthermore, Floride was anxious, for a time at least, to stay near her mother.

~ III ~

By the spring of 1810, the United States had been doubled in size by the purchase by Jefferson of the vast territories to the west known as Louisiana. Napoleon had retaken this area from Spain in the hope of permanently occupying that part of the world. Reverses in the Indies made him give up the idea, and Jefferson seized the opportunity. It was a vital period in the growth of his beloved Union, and Calhoun found himself more and more caught up in politics. He had had only nine weeks' experience in his State Legislature and had been a party to but two important bits of legislation, but his reputation had spread and now he had a seat in the Twelfth Session of the United States Congress.

Somehow, Timothy Dwight's remark made many years ago that Calhoun was good material for President kept recurring to him. It was an impossible dream, perhaps, but he couldn't get it out of his mind. His political experience was limited, and here in the National Congress

40

were not only young men of equal eagerness but older men of more genuine experience. An old friend of his, William Lowndes, was the same age but had had a year's experience in Congress, and another friend, Langdon Cheves, was six years older, as was Henry Clay, later to be known as "The Great Compromiser." Daniel Webster, the same age as himself, had only just joined the Federal Congress, and Calhoun soon realized that he would be a bitter opponent. He was from New Hampshire and a strong anti-administration man. There were others, both friends and political foes, but John had inherited a stubbornness from his father, and experience and age were of no account as opposition when a principle was at stake.

In 1811, four years after he had written and delivered the protest in the Chesapeake affair, impressment of American seamen by the British was still going on. Henry Clay, who had been elected Speaker, put John on the committee for Foreign Relations. The question of war with England, which had arisen in 1807, was still demanding an answer, and John Calhoun, with the authority of his new position, seized the opportunity of giving that answer. On December 12, 1811, he rose to reply to John Randolph of Virginia, who had expressed opposition to war.

His natural shyness made him a little fearful of speaking out for the first time in the National Congress. There were those in the room who would be listening critically to this young lawyer from South Carolina. Calhoun was well aware of it, but once on his feet, he spoke out in a firm voice in defense of his theories about the war.

He admitted that, at the moment, the nation was quite unprepared for war. This being the case, the first step, logically, was to start immediate preparation, since it was generally admitted that the war was justifiable. He attacked most vigorously the theory that the high taxes necessary to conduct the war would be out of proportion to the value of any ends to be attained. He protested "against this low and calculating avarice entering this hall of legislation. It is only fit for shops and counting houses." He sarcastically referred to the opposition's complete disregard of the fundamental cause for war. The British had persistently violated the rights of American citizens which the government was formed to protect. The loss in liberty and even life of the impressed seamen should not be valued in dollars and cents, he said. Their liberty and their lives were the responsibility of the government.

He was greeted by a round of applause from the Republicans, especially Henry Clay, who was as eager for war as was Calhoun, and a number of other young members whose warlike enthusiasm earned them the name "War Hawks." The situation was growing tense. All that was needed was the support of President Madison. In June of 1812, that support was secured by Clay as Speaker. He asked the President directly for an opinion. In his message, Madison said: "It is a solemn question which the Constitution wisely confides in the legislative department of the government. In recommending it to their early deliberation, I am happy in the assurance that the decision will be worthy of the enlightened and patriotic councils of a virtuous, a free and a powerful nation."

This was all Calhoun and the other War Hawks needed. The committee on foreign affairs issued its report recommending an immediate appeal to arms. The final bill, with a few amendments, was passed by both the House and Senate, and the infant United States was at war with the greatest sea power in the world.

Then a mysterious turn of Fate brought on another crisis. The day before Congress declared war, England had eased her restrictions; but since it took weeks for news to travel over the ocean, the principles of the embargo were continued. The New England antiwar element pointed out that the embargo had not prevented war after all, and the separatists had plenty of fuel for their arguments. The Reverend Timothy Dwight, in a violent sermon, likened New England to the children of Israel caught in the grip of the Egyptians.

In this very serious situation, Langdon Cheves proposed a bill to lighten the trade restrictions on New England for a limited time. In the discussion, it was proposed by Richardson of Massachusetts that the bill be amended to lighten the trade restrictions permanently rather than for a limited time. Although Cheves, who had offered the original bill, was a close friend and fellow Carolinian, Calhoun voted in favor of the Massachusetts amendment. He saw clearly the possibility of a break-up of the Union were New England to secede, and the shattering of the American dream. There was also a principle at stake, that of the rights of a minority. Without hesitation, he voted against his own party. The amendment, however, was not passed.

The war that Calhoun had been instrumental in declaring was not by any means unanimously approved. In his mind and in those of the War Hawks and many sympathizers in Congress, it was necessary if the newly established Union was to maintain any dignity or permanence and not be reduced again to colonial status. On the other hand, as Calhoun had told Randolph in no uncertain terms, the opponents' position was based solely on immediate inconvenience and material cost. It was incomprehensible to Calhoun that the greatest opposition came from New England, the progenitor of American independence. Greed, he felt, had taken the place of patriotism.

The war was carried on in widely separated sections of the continent. The conquest of Canada was the goal of many, who visualized new territory for settlement. Others concentrated on ridding the northwestern territory of British forts, and the Great Lakes became the scene of many naval battles. Twenty-nine-year-old Oliver Hazard Perry, who had distinguished himself in the war with the Barbary pirates, won a battle of broadsides over the British on Lake Erie, where he is said to have made the famous remark "We have met the enemy and they are ours." This and other victories were heartening to Calhoun and the War Hawks. He continued his encouragement of enlistments and the building of new frigates. He explained the invasion of Canada on the ground that it was a diversion to divide the British forces. This was quite sound as long as Napoleon was on the rampage in Europe, but by April, 1814, his mastery of the world faded into an unfulfilled dream and England was able, at least momentarily, to turn her attention to her obstreperous former colonies. Reinforcements arrived from across the sea, blockades were set up and the coast of America was ravaged. The people of Calhoun's home state of South Carolina lived in a state of terror as the older citizens remembered how, thirty years before, Tarleton's cavalry had devastated the land on their march to Charleston. But the British had bigger game in sight, and in August, 1814, they marched north to Washington, burnt the Capitol and all important buildings and, after feasting on a dinner prepared for the President and his charming Dolly, who had fled the city, set fire to the White House.

It looked hopeless for American Independence, but Calhoun kept up his spirits on the optimism of the old adage that "the flood tide follows the ebb." He privately felt, however, that defeat was imminent. Then, out of the west, came a long, lanky, ill-dressed frontiersman named Andrew Jackson. Enraged by the slaughter of 250 Americans by the Creek Indians, he invaded their territory and forced a treaty from them. Then, hearing that the British had entered Spanish Florida and were recruiting Creek refugees to help carry on the war from there, he entered Spanish territory without orders from the government and captured Pensacola. He was then ordered to proceed to

New Orleans, which the British were planning to seize in order to control the Mississippi River. In a battle fought on the left bank, Jackson defeated the British force so decisively that four generals and over 2,000 men of all ranks were killed. The army retreated to their transports, and the anticipated collapse of the young nation was miraculously prevented.

Calhoun was, of course, overjoyed. In his opinion the war—although rife with reverses, including the partial destruction of the Capitol—had brought all sections, even lukewarm New England, into one harmonious whole and strengthened the bonds of an ideal Union. "I feel pleasure and pride—that I am of a party that drew the sword," he said. His enthusiasm and that of the war party was thoroughly understandable. There was no denying that the prestige of the young United States was enhanced in the eyes of the world. The irony of it was that the slaughter at New Orleans was totally unnecessary. Peace had been signed three weeks before, on Christmas Eve.

Throughout over two years of devastating defeats and partial victories, Calhoun sat in the House faced with a myriad of issues—most, of course, brought on by the war, some vital and some insignificant. He was constantly harassed by bitter opponents, such as Randolph, Webster and Grosvenor. Of these, Daniel Webster of New Hampshire, the same age as himself, swarthy and broad-shouldered, was the newest and, Calhoun soon found out, perhaps the bitterest. He possessed a fluency in speaking that much impressed Calhoun but did not in the least disturb him. Since the success of his maiden speech he felt confidence in his own ability to cope with any situation, however forceful his opponent might be. Shortly after the opening of the Twelfth Session of Congress, he had a chance to exercise this confidence.

Rather brashly for a new member, Webster offered a motion very critical of the administration. He had already expressed his opinion very forcibly to a friend, saying after he had first met Madison, "I do not like his looks any more than his administration." This particular motion had to do with the revocation of the Berlin and Milan decrees, which France had originated in 1806–07 to blockade English shipping. England had offered to end her Orders in Council, aimed at stopping all shipping to France and her allies, a measure that had resulted in the President's authorizing an embargo on all vessels. Webster had it firmly in his mind that in some way Madison had suppressed the knowledge of the French action in order to have a motive for war with England. He phrased the motion in a very abrupt way, demanding that the President tell the Congress precisely "how, when and by whom" the knowledge was received. Calhoun listened in astonishment. In the first place, he himself was one of the chief instigators of the war, and he knew from firsthand contact that if such a revocation had been made by the French, there was absolutely no record of it in Washington. Actually, it was not known until three weeks after the declaration of war. Furthermore, the French had

interned American ships, which was not in accord with
any revocation of decrees and Orders in Council. What
disturbed Calhoun more, perhaps, was the violent attack
by an American on his President. The war was not going
too well, but it was going on, presenting every day most
practical problems, and Calhoun decided that further
argument on such a vague subject would be a waste of
time. President Madison could quite easily and truthfully
refute any accusation that Webster, stirred by his violent
opposition both to the administration and to the war,
could bring up, and Calhoun let the matter drop. At this
point, Webster said to a friend, "We had a warm time of
it for four days, and then the other side declined further
discussion." He did not admit defeat.

During the war, the manufacturers of the country had
grown in number largely through the needs of the war,
and they had been given protection from foreign competition by the restrictive system, a general name for embargo and nonimportation. Calhoun, being primarily a
planter, had always felt that the agriculturalist was handicapped by restricted shipping, since it was really a matter of indifference to him what the nationality of the
shipper might be. In June, 1812, in a long speech on the
suspension of nonimportation, he had spoken directly on
the general subject:

The restrictive system as a mode of resistance and
a means of obtaining redress of our wrongs has never
been a favorite one with me. I object to it for the

following reasons: because it does not suit the genius of our people, or that of our government, or the geographical character of our country. We are a people essentially active—distance and difficulties are less to us than to any people on earth. No passive system can suit such a people. Nor does it suit the genius of our government. Our government is founded on freedom and hates coercion.

Again, on April 6, 1814, as chairman of the Foreign Relations Committee, he spoke against the system, urging its repeal and the substitution of duties to protect the manufacturing interests. He pointed out that events had changed since the system was inaugurated, and that "persistence in the restrictive system was not the dictate of either wisdom or sound policy." Shortly after this, he was taken ill and was absent from the House for several days, but on April 14 he had the great satisfaction of hearing that the restrictive system had been repealed. It was the culmination of two years of deep thought and wearisome Congressional debate, and it strengthened him both physically and spiritually.

Arriving late in Washington, he had taken his seat in the midst of one of the stormiest debates in many years. Alexander J. Dallas, the Secretary of the Treasury, had offered a plan for the organization of a Second National Bank. The First National Bank, organized by Alexander Hamilton in 1791, had been discontinued in 1811. Dallas' plan envisioned a bank capitalized by the government to the extent of $20,000,000, part in specie but with the larger part in bank stock. The government was authorized to borrow money to carry on the war as soon as the capital had been secured.

Calhoun had never had much interest in or knowledge of banking. He was, generally speaking, in favor of some central authority through which to secure money to relieve the alarming financial situation in the country. His unfamiliarity with business, however, made him hesitate to express any opinion publicly, and the only solution was to give the whole thing careful study. After days and nights of concentrated research and thought and many conferences with Secretary Dallas, he offered a counter-measure. In his very practical way of thinking, he felt that the proposed arrangement obligated the government to issue stock on which it would pay a large interest, and then to borrow back the money at further interest. It seemed to him that the solution was to issue treasury notes, which would be paid from the sale of the bank's own stock. He realized only too well that he was going against the administration and many of his own party, but he made up his mind to go through with his plan and offer it in opposition.

This was in September, 1814, shortly before the war ended, and for the next few months the matter was hotly debated. It was Dallas versus Calhoun, with frequent concessions on both sides, but a final bill was lost four times, three times by a single vote and once by a Presidential veto. Calhoun had worked hard, and by January,

1815, his nerves were near the breaking point. He felt that by insisting on his plan, he was simply prolonging the bad state of financial affairs, and he was beginning to feel that he must concede something to others or no bill would result. Samuel Smith of Maryland and Daniel Webster of New Hampshire both emphasized the necessity of specie payment rather than the Treasury notes which were favored by Calhoun. When the bill was lost for the fifth time, he crossed the aisle to where Webster, his chief opponent, was sitting and begged his help in framing a new bill.

After the final session of the Thirteenth Congress, Calhoun returned to his plantation on the Savannah. He had fought hard and long for principles in which he believed, and he felt sincerely that he had been generally successful and that a Bank Bill would, before long, be enacted. Furthermore, the war was over and the infant United States had increased its prestige in the world. He looked forward to seeing his young son, Andrew Pickens, who was born just before the war, and his daughter, Floride, who was almost a year old. Even in the midst of his political activities, he never lost his love for a planters' life, and now he would have a chance to indulge himself. He had been home barely ten days when his dream was abruptly ended. Little Floride was well and happy when he reached Bath. One night she fell ill. Frantically John rode to the nearest doctor, who had his office in the next town. Attempts to ease the child's violent coughing were futile, and little Floride died before morning. The shock was

emphasized by the suddenness of the tragedy. He wrote
at once to his mother-in-law.

My dear Mother, Floride wrote to you by Mr.
Shackleford that all were well. We at that time little
calculated that in three days we should experience
the heaviest calamity that has ever occurred to us.
It is no less than the death of our interesting and
dearest daughter. She was in the bloom of health on
Wednesday morning, the 6th inst. and was a corps[e]
the next day. She was taken with a vomiting and
fever very suddenly about eleven o'clock and died
about an hour by sun the next morning. —So fixed in
sorrow is her distressed mother that every topick of
consolation which I attempt[t] to offer but seems to
grieve her the more—She thinks only of her dear
child and recalls to her mind everything that made
her interesting thus furnishing additional food for
her grief.

   We will expect you up as soon as your business
will permit. Floride desires her love to you. Our re-
spects to all friends.

                    I am with affection yours &
                         John C. Calhoun.

~ IV ~

The blow was great, and he wanted to stay at Bath to be of help to Floride; but Congressional business was a demanding obligation at this time of crisis. In late November, 1815, he set out for Washington. At Raleigh, North Carolina, he ran into the aging John Taylor of Virginia, politician and author. The two had a warm friendship, despite a difference of thirty years in their ages. Calhoun enjoyed the company of older men. It brought back pleasant memories of his childhood, when he had sat at his father's knee and listened to reminiscence of Indian Wars and violent expressions of opinions on public affairs. Calhoun and Taylor decided to take the new steam packet to Washington, the offspring of Robert Fulton's *Clermont*, which had made such a sensation on the Hudson River in 1807. At this early stage in the development of steam boats, it was a rather crude affair. The accommodations were very limited, and the noise of the engines and the smells from the engine room were hard to bear. But it

moved smoothly along the coast, and was certainly to be
preferred to the rough and dangerous roads ashore. Talking with Taylor served to distract Calhoun's mind from
his sorrow. The older man was most sympathetic when
Calhoun told him of Floride's death, and tactfully turned
the conversation to other channels. He was a Southerner,
a strong states' rights man and a firm believer in Jeffersonian principles. Although a Virginian, he had not joined
his state in ratifying the Constitution, feeling that the
rights of states and individuals were not sufficiently protected. On these subjects the two men had much in common, but in the matter of the recent war their viewpoints
differed.

"I feel, John," Taylor argued, "that when a country in-
dulges in a war, the strength of the central government is
increased, and that I don't want to see."

Calhoun, as one of the chief instigators of the war, gave
a most logical answer. "I agree with you," he said, "in ob-
jecting to too strong a central government, but in this
case we needed strength. We are a new country, and we
had to take a firm stand. Strength is what we needed.
Otherwise, we might easily have lost all that our Revolution stood for."

Taylor thought this over, "All wars," he replied, ignor-
ing the logic, "tend to destroy that 'pursuit of happiness'
which all men are entitled to."

"If a war brings justice, it creates happiness," Calhoun
answered in a tone that was definitely final. Personal worries were recurring to him. He had lost faith in country

doctors, since one had failed him in his recent tragedy. He decided that if Floride should have another child, she must go to Charleston when the time approached.

The session opened on December 4, 1815, and he found himself made chairman of the Committee on Uniform Currency. This was undoubtedly due to his prominence in the National Bank discussions at the previous sessions, but it rather amused him when he thought of how recently he had given little, if any, attention to money matters. It was, however, a definite sign of his growing prestige in governmental matters, and he was proud of it, even admitting to himself at times to a little conceit.

The issues in 1816 were not new; they simply had not yet been resolved, and a fresh approach was badly needed. In Calhoun's mind, they could all be tied up in one package and labeled "Save the Union."

The three most vital issues to him were a protective tariff, a central bank and a system of roads and canals. His thoughts on the tariff were far different from those he would fight for twelve years later, but conditions were vastly different then and, as usual, he was acting logically under existing circumstances. The manufacturers of New England who had prospered during the war were losing money to the East India cotton trade. The logical answer was some form of tariff protection. To Calhoun, it was axiomatic that they had a right to it. The development of American capital was being handicapped not only in New England but as far south as the Carolinas; the scattered cotton mills were fast falling by the wayside; Pittsburgh,

with its iron deposits, was unable to meet the competition
of British coke-iron or the charcoal iron from Sweden;
in Vermont and Ohio, the sheepherders were protesting
against the import of British wool. There was definite
danger that the infant Union, which had so recently de-
monstrated its integrity as an independent nation, would
soon become subservient to the rest of the world. Calhoun
spoke boldly in the Senate, answering logically all the
vituperative objections offered by such men as Webster
and Randolph. A tariff would, he insisted, help bind together the scattered parts of the Union and thus prevent
what he most feared—disunion. Although he was not actually on the committee that drew up the final tariff bill,
he had so strongly defended it that he was conscious of
a certain personal success when, on April 27, 1816, the
new tariff went into effect with President Madison's sig-
nature. Thus one part of his "package" was achieved.
Would he succeed with the other two—the bank problem
and internal improvements?

His youthful enthusiasm would not permit the defeat
of the bank bill at the last session to discourage him.
Something had to be done. The currency of the country
was a shambles. Paper money in one state was worthless
in another, and state banks took it upon themselves to
refuse loans quite arbitrarily. With the Constitution as
his guiding star, Calhoun insisted that the government
alone had the power to "coin money and regulate the
value thereof." With Webster's help and considerable
concession on his own part, a bill was finally passed and

the Second National Bank established. It was, in a sense, his bank, and this was pretty generally admitted. His persistence, his generosity in giving in here and there and the thoughtful clarity of his views made him the real sponsor. Many critics in and out of Congress had said that the bank had no right to issue currency. In their opinion, this was the function of each sovereign state. This theory did not fit in with Calhoun's idea of a compact union, and he spoke most forcibly against it. He was still holding fast to his nationalist theories, not yet being fully conscious of changing conditions that might alter his thinking. He had consistently insisted that "the present state of our circulating medium is opposed to the principle of our Federal Constitution. The power is given in that instrument in express terms 'to coin money, to regulate the value thereof and of foreign coin'. . . ." Under the existing circumstances, he was right, but in his support of the tariff and then the bank he was, unbeknownst to himself, oiling a machine that was destined to crush his hopes for a perfect union.

A short visit to Bath renewed his spirits, and he returned to Washington to fight for the third item in his "package"—internal improvements.

This was the question of roads and canals. President Madison was about to leave office at the end of his term, and in his final message to Congress he said: ". . . And I particularly invite, again, your attention to the expediency of exercising their powers—and, where necessary, of resorting to the prescribed mode of enlarging them in

order to effectuate a comprehensive system of roads and
canals. . . ."

With the Speaker of the House firmly on his side, and
now the President, Calhoun felt no doubt that the last
step would bring him to his goal—a firm Union. It would
complete what Henry Clay termed the American System,
a protective tariff for the manufacturers and a home market and better transportation for the farmers. In intro-
ducing the bill for internal improvements, he spoke with
confidence in its success.

"We are greatly and rapidly—I was about to say fear-
fully—growing. This is our pride and our danger, our
weakness and our strength. Let us bind the Republic together with a perfect system of roads and canals. Protection would make the parts adhere more closely—it
would form a most powerful cement."

At the time he spoke, he was quite justified in expressing a certain fear. The growth he mentioned had statis-
tically shown a 100 per cent increase since the War of
1812 in the country west of the Appalachians, and the
population spiral was not decreasing.

Calhoun was fully aware that most of the opposition
to the "Roads and Canals" bill was based on what the
critics called its unconstitutionality, and he tactfully
phrased the bill so as to appear to be offering Congress
the chance to use its judgment and possible Constitutional amendments in considering the issue. His entire
approach was to prove the value of the roads and canals
not only to the economy of the country and possible mili-

tary movements but also to the preservation of unity among so vast a number of scattered inhabitants. Just before the question on the bill was called for, he delivered a long speech on all these points.

He praised the enterprise, strength and courage of the American people, but he pointed out the vastness of the territory they occupied—greater, he said, than ever occupied by a free people and way out of proportion to their numbers—and he warned that its very size was a threat to their liberty and union. Unless some method was found to bring the scattered parts together, complete disunion would be sure to follow. He ended with his proposal: "Let us bind the Republic together with a perfect system of roads and canals. Let us conquer space."

Four days later, the bill was passed and sent to President Madison barely a month before he was to leave office. It was not exactly the bill Calhoun had hoped for. It was altered by many amendments, the most vital of which was inserted by Timothy Pickering. By it the permission of a state would have to be secured before any road could be built across it. But Calhoun was happy about it. The bonds of union were tightened and, together with the incentive to individual initiative given by the tariff and the national bank, he saw his dream of liberty and union becoming a reality.

Late in February, he went to the White House to formally say good-bye to President Madison. The two men sat together for some time. Calhoun congratulated the President on the success of his administration, especially mentioning the tariff, the bank and the proposed internal improvements. Madison thanked him for his excellent work in the House. The conversation touched on many common interests, and soon Calhoun took his leave. He had just reached the door when the President called him back. "Mr. Calhoun," he said, and there was a slight note of apology in his voice, "you mentioned just now the proposed internal improvements. I am fully aware of how ably and sincerely you fought for the bill just passed by Congress and now lying on my desk, but I find, after careful consideration, too many possible Constitutional problems which need more study. I am afraid I shall have to veto it at this time." There was a moment's silence. Calhoun could think of no appropriate words. Here, suddenly, one-third of his "package" was lost. He realized, though, that Madison was merely exercising the right and duty of the Chief Executive. He thanked him for giving the matter detailed thought and left the White House.

He had suffered a political disappointment just before the end of the session, but he had personal news that made the defeat easier to bear. He had not had a letter from Floride for a long time, and as he wrote home most religiously himself, he was much concerned. Floride was not a good letter writer, but the long silence was hard to understand until he received word that he had a new daughter, and both Floride and the baby were quite well. This was particularly happy news for him. Ever since little Floride's death in 1815, he had felt the loss desperately. Now it was as if she had been reincarnated, and he silently thanked God. He wrote at once to Floride expressing his happiness.

The Fourteenth Session of Congress was over, and he was ready to go home to Floride at Bath. The veto of one of his pet bills, so completely unexpected, had been a hard blow to take. There was some consolation, though, in looking back over the Twelfth, Thirteenth and Fourteenth sessions. He was only thirty-five years old, and he had had not only a share but great influence in the passing of most vital legislation, and had achieved a reputation and respect that few men of his age could claim.

Aside from the matter of the veto, there was another cause of some concern. During the session, a bill had been introduced to raise the pay of Congressmen to $1,500 a year. Calhoun had not only favored the bill but suggested a higher annual pay, even up to $2,500. The measure was not too popular in the country, and his additional suggestion alienated many of his former supporters. It was widely rumored that he would lose his seat in Congress at the next election. This was definitely a cause for worry, but not for changing his mind. His convictions on principle were permanent, and in this case were based on the responsibility of being a Congressman and the increasing cost of transportation. Also, he personally regretted the long periods of separation from home and family which his job required. He saw clearly the possibility of defeat, but he made up his mind that he would offer himself as a candidate, explain the reasons for his vote calmly and logically and simply await results. Many of the members who were in favor of the motion thought the situation too explosive and refused to stand for re-election. Calhoun, however, toured his districts, meeting objections with quiet logic and refusing to offer the slightest apology for his action in the matter of salary raise. Gossip and prejudice were rampant, but when the votes were counted, he was returned triumphantly to the Fifteenth Session of Congress. He was most happy with Floride, his son Andrew and his latest child, and looked forward to more years of success in Congress. Occasionally, the casual prophecy of Timothy Dwight made thirteen years before crept into his consciousness, only to be dismissed with a faint smile.

Then, on October 10, 1817, he received a letter from President Monroe asking that he accept the office of Secretary of War in the new Cabinet. The President's choice had fallen on Calhoun after careful consideration of five other possibilities, including Henry Clay and William Lowndes. There were very sound reasons for the choice. Monroe himself had held the office temporarily in 1814 after the fall of Washington. He and Calhoun had frequently discussed military matters, and found that they held similar views. Furthermore, ever since his War Hawk days, Calhoun had stressed the need of defense against invasion. In 1816 he had said, "I am sure that future wars with England are not only possible but are highly probable." This thought of defense had even colored his thinking on such issues as the tariff and the national bank. When he urged protection for woolens and cotton, he had in mind material for army uniforms. Monroe deemed him a most natural choice.

Calhoun gave the offer a brief but intense consideration, and on November 1, 1817, he wrote the President: ". . . I am impressed with the importance of the trust which you have tendered to me, and in determining to accept it, I am governed by a sincere desire to add to the prosperity of the country and the reputation of your administration." He resigned from the House. Many of his friends criticized him for not remaining in Congress, where he was exercising such great influence, but he saw in his new assignment an opportunity to work towards his ideal—an adequate defense of the Union. This was his nationalism. The bill for the construction of roads and canals had been defeated by a veto, but he hoped that perhaps this essential part of his ideal might be achieved from his new position.

Before Calhoun could seriously consider any national problems, he was faced with a small personal one. All through his career in Congress, he had spent his time between sessions with his family on the Savannah River. He had always looked forward to these returns to plantation life, from which he had never really freed himself— the friendly greetings from his slaves, particularly his old fishing companion, Sawney, the smell of the rich, black earth and the growing things breaking through it into the sunshine. He even occasionally took a hand at the plow. Now, with the more permanent work of his new office, he would have to stay in Washington.

Accordingly, he rented a house on E Street, and soon was established there with his wife and two children. Calhoun had wanted his new daughter to be called Floride, but was overruled by his wife, who was a little fearful of any constant reminder of the daughter she had lost. They settled on the name Anna Marie. Although he didn't know it, this new little daughter was to be a source of strength to him for the rest of his life. Floride, with her graciousness and warmth of manner, very soon made friends. Together with her now-famous husband, she established the house on E Street as a mecca for the elite of Washington. The tall, rather stern but handsome new Secretary of War and his vivacious Huguenot wife hosted many a ball and dinner attended by members of all political beliefs. After all, it was the "Era of Good Feeling." Napoleon was safely isolated on the island of Elba busily writing excuses for his years of plunder, the activities of the Holy Alliance appeared to be limited to Europe and the future seemed reasonably bright.

Knowing very well that his knowledge of military matters was limited, Calhoun decided that, rather than do anything drastic at once, he would simply listen to complaints and suggestions. There were plenty of both. The economy of the Military was in chaos. Discipline was almost nonexistent, rules for conduct being different on every one of the widely scattered army posts. Orders were frequently issued over the heads of superior officers, and there was no one to whom the offended officer could complain. In February, 1815, Monroe had retired from his temporary tenure of the War Office after the burning of Washington, and until Calhoun took over in December, 1817, there was no really responsible head of the department.

In the matter of discipline, Calhoun found himself almost immediately in a rather delicate situation. The irascible General Jackson had actually made it clear that he would be personally responsible for the disobedience of orders by his subordinates, remarking casually that he was in favor of the refusal to obey orders. Three years before, when Jackson had marched into Spanish territory without orders, Calhoun had disapproved of his action, but had not been in a position to reprimand him. Now he was in that position, and a reprimand was obviously called for.

Calhoun had a problem. He had great respect for the violent old general, and the possibility of losing him was a distinct deterrent to any very radical official action. He called upon all his available tact, which in vital matters was considerable, and after reminding Jackson of the necessity of complete respect for field orders, he continued, "I am persuaded that no one is more deeply concerned of the truth of this proposition than yourself, and it is only necessary to call your attention to the irregularities which I have stated to relieve me from the necessity of determining whether I shall permit the orders of the government to be habitually neglected or resort to the proper means of enforcing them. Should the alternative be presented, I will not hesitate to do my duty." At

a later time, when Jackson was engaged in putting down
an insurrection of the Florida Seminoles and marched
without orders into Spanish territory, Calhoun suggested
in a Cabinet meeting that the general be court-martialed.

Aside from altercations with Jackson, his relations with
the government were, in general, most pleasant, but he
missed not having a part in Congressional discussions.
The country was faced with many vital issues in which
he had an intense interest, but his relations with Congress
were, of course, confined to Senator Willams of the Military Affairs Committee. Their constant meetings and discussions proved most successful in straightening out the
turbulent affairs of the War Department. Not only was
the extraordinary deficit of $45,000,000 almost wiped out,
but changes were made in fundamental organization, and
such was Calhoun's popularity that these changes were
made with the cooperation of most ranking field officers.
A board of responsible heads of each department was
established in Washington with final authority in all matters pertaining to each particular branch. One of Calhoun's schemes was to reduce the number of men in the
ranks from 10,000 to 6,000 while retaining the whole of
the staff of experienced officers. By this move he planned
to cut down the army's expenses without lessening its
fundamental potential in case of war. In 1802, Jefferson
had established West Point as a purely engineering
school, but Calhoun reorganized it as a general military
academy under the leadership of General Sylvanus
Thayer. All these changes met with the approval of rank-

ing army officers, who felt the strength, considerateness and cooperation of their new chief, a feeling that had never existed under the old scattered and undisciplined system.

Then, in October, 1819, his family was increased by the birth of another daughter, whom they named Elizabeth. Calhoun loved children. His friends always remarked that he was stern only with older people. As a child, he had never had playmates, and it was as though he were making up for lost time.

Calhoun's popularity was growing but, politics being what it has always been, the road ahead was not to be consistently smooth. There was jealousy of this young aspiring war secretary. Monroe's term of office would soon end, the coveted office of President would be wide open and popularity would bring votes. Politicians reacted in the usual way. Calhoun was deluged with carping questions of relative unimportance, his requests for essential appropriations were drastically cut, there were constant disputes about army regulations, his forward-looking scheme for reducing the rank and file was virtually ignored and at one time he was actually accused of profiting from an army contract. Calhoun, of course, knew the reason for all this, and he was also aware that there was a basis for jealousy. He did hope for the Presidency, a hope shared by each of his critics on his own behalf. As a member of Monroe's Cabinet, he felt his chances were good, but he also knew that there were more experienced men in the government, possibly with better claims. There was the great war hero Andrew Jackson, John Q. Adams, a close friend, Speaker Henry Clay and Secretary of the Treasury William H. Crawford, of the so-called radical party (made up of Jeffersonian democrats, strict construction ists and states' rights adherents). Calhoun realized that his age was against him, but the thought hovered on.

Then a very simple routine matter came before Congress. Missouri, a part of the Louisiana land purchase, asked to be admitted as a state. James Talmadge, Jr., of New York proposed an amendment to the bill, asking that before statehood was officially granted, the further introductions of slaves into the territory be forbidden. These were simple words with some logic behind them, but they were pregnant with terrifying possibilities. Old Thomas Jefferson wrote that "the Missouri question arouses and fills me with alarm." The matter was hotly discussed for months, and in January, 1820, a compromise bill was passed by House and Senate. Missouri was to be admitted as a slaveholding state, but thereafter slavery was to be prohibited in the territory of the United States north of the latitude 36″ 30°. A geographical line was thus drawn between North and South, between slave and antislave—an ominous division. Calhoun discussed the matter in his many talks with Adams. His conclusion was that the whole matter was purely political, and he saw no danger of a dissolution of the Union, the one thing at the time that he most dreaded.

In March, 1820, little Elizabeth died of a pulmonary

weakness that seemed to be a family characteristic. Calhoun himself suffered from it. Grief-stricken, he braced himself against any sort of collapse. His responsibility to the country was a demanding task.

~ V ~

The political undercurrents that were disturbing the otherwise smooth surface of War Department activities increased as Monroe's second term opened. The South Carolina legislature, a little dubious of Crawford's chances for election, asked Calhoun if he would allow his name to be used as a possible candidate for the Presidency. Here was Timothy Dwight's prophecy emerging from a dream into the world of reality, and he promptly agreed. For a time, he made no personal effort, but the next year, with the help of friends, he established *The Washington Republican* to publicly present his views and combat Crawfords' paper, *The City Gazette,* adopting the motto "Libertas et natale solum" (Liberty and my native land). For a time, the paper was well received, and his hopes ran high. Then two events altered the situation. Shortly after the paper began publication, William Lowndes, a serious candidate, died, and William Crawford called a caucus, a method of electioneering not altogether popular. In this meeting, Crawford was defeated. This left only two candidates in the running besides Calhoun—Adams and Jackson. He considered the situation carefully. Both men were older and more experienced, and one was a national hero. It seemed to him that his chances were rather slim, and after all he had youth in his favor and could wait. He announced in his *Republican* that he was withdrawing from the contest. He did this with great reluctance, for he had, for a time, seemed so near his goal. There was, however, some consolation. He was nominated for Vice President by the adherents of both Adams and Jackson, and even Webster, who was so often a bitter opponent, said of him, "He is a true man, and will do good to the country in that situation." He received the majority of the electoral votes, including practically all of New England.

This was, of course, complimentary and a definite step towards the Presidency, but it rather concerned him because of his relations with the two men. Adams was a long-time friend who had praised Calhoun on many occasions. When Monroe appointed him to the post of War Secretary, Adams had said most sincerely, "Calhoun is a man of fair and candid mind—of enlarged philosophic views and of ardent patriotism." But when he found himself facing Calhoun as a dangerous rival for the position he coveted, his attitude changed, and Calhoun felt that it might be difficult to work with him as Vice President. As for Jackson, Calhoun had a warm feeling for the violent old "man of the people" in spite of his public

criticism of him, and Jackson, not yet having heard of
Calhoun's court-martial suggestion, felt nothing but
friendship for him. After all, they were both Democrats
at heart. Which way would the wind blow?

As Calhoun had feared, the electoral vote was 99 for
Jackson and 89 for Adams, throwing the election into the
lap of Congress. Having received the majority of the popular vote, Jackson was jubilantly on his way to Washington to be inaugurated. He was doomed to disappointment. The House, under the sway of Henry Clay, voted
in favor of John Q. Adams, who was duly elected President with John C. Calhoun as Vice President.

Shortly before the election, Calhoun moved his family,
now increased by Cornelia, Patrick and little John Bonneau, from the E Street house to the heights above
Georgetown. The air was clearer than in the center of
Washington. As young John had not been well, it was
thought the change might benefit him. The move was
expensive, and he had to accept help from Floride's
mother. His *Republican* had been a popular but rather
costly enterprise. Then, in early 1826, John grew worse
and they were forced to rush him South. He finally recovered, and the Calhouns decided to keep the family in
Bath, and rent or board when in Washington.

Inaugurated on March 4, 1825, Calhoun found himself, as he had feared, in a rather awkward position. His
personal relations with Adams had not essentially improved since his first declaration of his candidacy, and
politically the two men did not exactly see eye to eye.

They were physically a somewhat ill-assorted pair: Adams was short, stout and bald-headed, while his handsome Vice President was over six feet with thick wavy hair and piercing blue eyes. Temperamentally, they also differed. Many people respected John Q. Adams, but few had any real affection for him. There was a prejudiced curtness about his handling of any issue, and his interest in matters in general was more political then genuinely constructive.

As president of the Senate, Calhoun had a definite task that did not conflict too closely with Adams. His future seemed bright. Jackson was almost certain to succeed Adams, and he had been assured of the Vice Presidency under the old war hero with the probability of succeeding him as President. He chose to do his duty quietly and with dignity, and await events.

Then, from an unexpected quarter, he had a new challenge. John Randolph, an aristocratic slaveholding Virginian and an intimate friend of Thomas Jefferson, had served in the House with Calhoun when the latter was a fledgling congressman. They had disagreed violently on many occasions. Calhoun, in one of his first speeches had brilliantly answered Randolph's opposition to the War of 1812. This was the beginning of Calhoun's reputation as a speaker, and the two had clashed many times after that. Now Randolph was in the Senate, and Calhoun, as Vice President, was the presiding officer. On March 30, 1826, Randolph chose to speak on a proposal by Adams to send a mission to Panama. As a member of the opposition, he

had a right to speak, but his manner of doing it was quite
out of order. He was normally a most gifted if violent
orator, but his age and intemperate habits had somewhat
distorted his oratorical gifts. The words flowed brilliantly
at times, but were blurred and confused at others. In
either case, their significance was unmistakable—almost
cruel criticism of President Adams and his Secretary of
State, Henry Clay. Randolph's harsh, somewhat falsetto
voice did not soften the viciousness of his words. There
was silent consternation in the Senate chamber, and
heads were turned towards the presiding officer. Calhoun
did nothing to stop the furious diatribe of the member
from Virginia, and the next day he found himself the
target of censure by the press for not calling Randolph
to order. South Carolina, on the other hand, praised him
as the champion of free debate. It seemed like a serious
blot on his heretofore meticulous handling of a difficult
position, but Calhoun was not particularly disturbed.
During Randolph's outburst he had seen the questioning
glances of the members, and had thought seriously of
calling him to order. He had, however, a logical answer
to his critics. He pointed out "that the right to call to
order belongs exclusively to the members of this body,
and not to the chair. The power of the presiding officer
is an appelate power only." His contention was, of course,
rejected by the opposition senators and most of the country's press but, in 1828 an amendment was passed giving
the presiding officer of the Senate the duty of calling a
member to order.

The four years of Adams' administration passed reasonably quietly for the Vice President. His position gave him ample time for reflection without responsibility. He had recently purchased a plantation at Pendleton, S.C., on the Seneca River. His lungs were not strong, and he found the somewhat elevated spot better for his breathing. It was not a pretentious establishment compared with many of the other Southern plantations, and there was no army of slaves, merely enough to take care of the modest cotton and corn fields. He was particularly happy in the spring, when the dogwood and jasmine were in bloom. From his house, the green fields extended to the bottomland by the Seneca River and to the north to forested slopes and the foothills of the Blue Ridge mountains. He named it Fort Hill because of a nearby ruined fortification built by a distant relative, General Pickens, as protection against the Cherokee Indians during the Revolution. It was an ideal spot to bring up his growing family, rest and think, and recent events had given him much to consider.

The talk of emancipation was growing, given impetus by the Talmadge amendment in the Missouri case, which fixed a geographical line between slave and nonslave states. The ever-increasing tariff spurred by Adams and the consequent indulgence given to northern industry were matters that alarmed him. Did it all mean an eventual breakup of the Union he had so enthusiastically and painstakingly defended all through his political life? Relations with England and the new South American republics were being handled and mishandled by Clay and Adams. Adams' proposal to send a commision to Panama met with Southern opposition, because the question of emancipation was sure to come up. Negroes were free in the southern republics, mulatto generals would obviously not be in sympathy with the opinion of the slaveholding states.

All these things confused Calhoun. At the time of the Missouri Compromise, he had belittled the danger of a sectional split solely on the issue of slavery and had favored the Compromise as an example of the working of a true democracy. "I can scarcely conceive," he wrote in 1820, "of a cause of sufficient power to divide the Union. . . . We to the South ought not to assent easily to the belief that there is a conspiracy against our property. . . . Nothing would lead more directly to disunion with all its horrors." He remembered how he had agreed with old John Taylor about the danger of too strong a central government. Was it possible, he pondered, that the Union might actually be divided into North and South and that the Northern government might become too strong and in some way oppress the South?

In the matter of the tariff proposed by Adams, which became known as "The Tariff of Abominations," Calhoun found himself in sympathy with the Southern point of view. The Southern states were primarily producers of raw materials, and in order to survive, they felt they must be able to sell them anywhere. The Southerners stated that they had no hostility to manufacturers, but saw no reason to grant them any particular privileges. Still struggling to be optimistic, Calhoun wrote to his friend Duff Gordon: "I cannot but think that the impression which exists in the minds of many of your virtuous and well-informed citizens to the south . . . that there has commenced between the North and the South a premeditated struggle for superiority, is not correct."

Being a man of extraordinarily fair mind, Calhoun was able to see something of rightness on both sides; he also refused to come out strongly for one or the other because he was Vice President in a weak administration that could scarcely be expected to continue for more than one term. The next President was almost sure to be the popular hero Andrew Jackson, who, after all, had been definitely the popular choice in 1824. Calhoun and Jackson were friendly at the moment, and it was tacitly assumed between them that since Jackson's health would hardly permit a second term, Calhoun would, in all probability, succeed him in the highest office. An aspiring candidate could hardly afford to antagonize one-half of the voters. Calhoun never for a moment denied to himself his political ambitions. After all, through his own skill and tolerance, he had won his way to the second highest position the country had to offer. Who could gainsay his right to covet the next step? Floride knew of this ambition, and also knew that his attitude towards slavery and the tariff was at the moment most sincere and not primarily influenced by political considerations. He loved the Union and dreaded, as he always had, any issue that would break it up. He would reconcile the Northern manufacturers with the agriculturalists of the South if this were at all possible, and he would never stop trying.

The end of the Adams term was fast approaching. There was little doubt in Calhoun's mind that he would be elected Vice President in the next administration, and he was able to concentrate on the problems brought up by Adams' "Tariff of Abominations." In Calhoun's mind, the protective tariff issue far outweighed the question of slavery. Jackson had not yet declared himself, but there was the hope that he would do so as President, and tone the bill down to revenue raising rather than superprotection. In the meantime, Calhoun decided to make his own position quite clear, and to do his best to secure support against the bill as it then stood. He faced the issue squarely, and told leaders who were working for his re-election that he saw only two roads to follow. The simpler was to elect Jackson. After all, he was a Southerner and, at the moment, uncommitted. The other was to have the Southern states veto the high-tariff bill. If this sounded too radical, he could cite precedents. Had not Virginia and Kentucky threatened in 1793 to veto the Alien and Sedition laws, and in 1809, Massachusetts had threatened secession over Jefferson's embargo. The present matter was vital, and desperate measures had to be taken. He summed up his fears in a letter to a friend. "The ground we have taken is that the tariff act is unconstitutional and must be repealed—that the rights of the South have been destroyed and must be restored—that the Union is in danger and must be saved," he wrote.

"No government," he said shortly after this, "based on the naked principle that the majority ought to govern . . . can preserve its liberty even for a single generation." These were bold words which brought up questions of constitutionality, states' rights and political prejudice, but he said them unhesitatingly through his ardent desire for a settlement that would not divide the Union. To those who claimed that this procedure was tantamount to actual secession, Calhoun replied that nullification did not imply secession any more than a disagreement between business partners implied a breakup in their relations. He had deemed the Missouri Compromise proper procedure in a democracy, and he was quite willing to compromise again. The fog of uncertainty that had blurred his thinking was clearing. He saw the road ahead—difficult, perhaps but, to his way of thinking, quite straight.

To nobody's surprise, Andrew Jackson was elected President. The frantic efforts of Webster and Clay could not save Adams from an ignominious defeat. After a campaign colored with some scandalous personal charges against both candidates, Jackson was clearly the people's choice by a very distinct majority. Calhoun, with only slightly fewer votes than Jackson, became Vice President, an interesting combination of Jeffersonian Republicanism and Jacksonian Democracy.

Preinauguration social events were curtailed somewhat because of the death of the President-elect's wife. Rachel Jackson had been an invalid for some time, but her death was a bitter blow to the rather sentimental old frontiersman—especially at the height of his political glory. On March 4, 1829, the inauguration took place. Pennsylvania Avenue, as usual, was muddy, but this did not prevent "Old Hickory," as his supporters called him, from walking to the ceremonies. He was accompanied by men who had served in the Revolution and were referred to by him as companions of the immortal Washington. At the East portico of the Capitol, the oath of office was administered by Chief Justice John Marshall, and Jackson made his inaugural address.

Tall, stately and rugged and dressed entirely in black with a heavy crepe arm band in memory of his beloved Rachel, the messiah of the common people turned and faced the almost hysterical crowd. Floride Calhoun watched her husband's face as Jackson began to speak. She knew what he was hoping to hear, and she prayed silently for a realization of his hopes. Calhoun listened to every word. He heard that the Constitution must be obeyed, states' rights observed and the Federal Union preserved. There was much said about paying the national debt and avoiding loans and direct taxes, but he listened in vain for any definite suggestion of lowering the tariff rates to a level of revenue only. References to the subject were vague and open to anyone's interpretation, and it seemed evident to him that he had supported the wrong man. The reference to states' rights was hollow, without mention of the tragic position of the South under crushing Northern protection. To preserve the Union and destroy the South was a paradox that passed his understanding. He would wait to see if the new President's actions would be more definite than his words and act according to his convictions.

The address finished, the presidential party adjourned to the White House for the usual reception—but there was nothing usual about it. Democracy swarmed over the White House. If your shoes were muddy, you wiped them on the carpet; if you couldn't see over the crowd, you stood on a satin-covered chair; and if the legs broke under your weight, you stood on something else. Since there were varying opinions, there were disputes, many ending in blackened eyes and bloodied noses. Finally, large bowls of punch were placed on the lawn as enticement to the crowd to leave the White House. Before too long, relative peace and quiet reigned. The "messiah" was on his throne.

After the riotous ceremonies were over, Calhoun had a steak dinner with the presidential party. He didn't enjoy it much because he was disturbed by the events of the afternoon. It was not only that his inherent Huguenot graciousness rebelled at the ill manners of the guests at the White House reception, but also that it all seemed so trivial in comparison with the real issues that were as yet unsettled. Frontiers were expanding almost daily, bringing up the question of representation in Congress

between Northern manufacturers and Southern agriculturalists; and foreign relations were in a state of flux, with
veiled threats from France and Spain. In Calhoun's mind,
the most immediate problem was the viciously high tariff
rates, which threatened the South and, further, the very
existence of the Union. In 1828, just prior to the election,
he had sent a report to the South Carolina legislators
stating his attitude towards the 1828 tariff and recommending a stand against it by all Southern states. This
was warmly debated, and resulted in a bill known as "Exposition and Protest Reported by the Special Committee
of the House Of Representatives" or, more commonly,
"The South Carolina Exposition." Although many of its
basic points were Calhoun's, his connection with it was
not yet made public. His position as Vice President was a
delicate one under the circumstances.

As the months went by, Calhoun felt his position becoming more and more delicate. There were unmistakable rumors flying about that he was the author of the
"Exposition." He couldn't help noticing in his meetings
with Jackson a certain coolness in the President's manner, as though he had heard the rumors and was secretly
suspicious of his Vice President. This distressed Calhoun,
as his relations with Jackson had been amicable if not
warm, and he wanted to keep them that way. This was
not only because he desperately wanted the President's
sympathy and cooperation in his struggle for the equality
of the South, but also because his own succession to the
Presidency depended very largely on it.

In January of 1830, Senator Robert Y. Hayne, a strong supporter of Calhoun, rose in the Senate to defend the South's attitude in the matter of the "Tariff of Abominations." He attacked the Government for "presuming to regulate the industry of man . . . and to reorganize the whole labor and capital of the country." His attack launched one of the bitterest debates the Senate had listened to in years. Daniel Webster took up the gauntlet for the North and the administration. As president of the Senate, Calhoun could only listen and control the decorum of the Senate chamber. When Webster cleverly turned the argument into a defense of patriotism it was painful for Calhoun to keep silent. His personal patriotism was to the Union of sovereign states, with liberty to speak and be heard. He knew perfectly well that Webster's patriotism was to a central authority that dominated and dictated to the several states—union without liberty.

Webster's confidently fluent speech went on for hours. The small galleries were packed; every eye was focused on the tall, dignified speaker in his neat blue coat, brass buttons and buff waistcoat. He was appealing to the sensitivity of his listeners if not always to logic. Calhoun listened attentively, balancing every word against his own convictions and sound logic. As he drew to his climax, Webster intoned: "It is to that Union that we owe our safety at home. . . ." "What safety?" Calhoun asked himself. "Was it the Union that was planning to destroy the economy and happiness of half its members?" Webster continued, almost carried away by poetic imagery.

When my eyes shall be turned to behold for the
last time the sun in heaven may I not see him shin-
ing on the broken and disfigured fragments of a once
glorious Union . . . on a land rent with civil feuds,
or drenched, it may be, in fraternal blood. . . . Let
their last feeble and lingering glance rather behold
the gorgeous ensign of the republic . . . bearing
for its motto not those words of delusion and folly,
Liberty first and Union afterwards, but everywhere,
spread all over in characters of living light, blazing
on all its ample folds, as they float over the sea and
over the land, and in every wind under the whole
heavens that other sentiment, dear to every true
American heart—Liberty and Union, now and forever, one and inseparable.

There was a moment of stunned silence, and then the
applause burst out, uncontrollable, from the pent-up
emotion brought on by the passionate oratory of the last
few hours. Calhoun joined, but he couldn't help noting
that Webster ended his peroration with the word "liberty" ahead of "Union." The debate was over. Both sides
had fired telling barrages at each other, but the indications were clearly that each held firmly to its position.
Webster was speaking for the administration, but were
his words wholly Jackson's considered opinion? He had
not yet come out decisively on the tariff question, and
Calhoun and his friends still hoped he might see the
South's side of the tariff threat. If Jackson was convinced

that Calhoun had largely formulated the "Exposition" which attacked his policies, the chances were that he would not give in. Jackson, Calhoun had come to know, was a man to whom personalities were more important than policies, and if his Vice President should oppose him, it was he who must suffer, however logical his opposition might be.

Calhoun clearly faced a vital dilemma that demanded a solution. As things stood at the moment, the South would be slowly strangled for the benefit of the North and West. Should he choose unquestioning loyalty to the administration and stand by to see half the Union impoverished, or should he hold to his convictions and find some way to realize them? The answer was not long in coming. Thomas Jefferson's eighty-seventh birthday was to be celebrated on April 13 with a Presidential dinner at Embree's Indian Queen Hotel. The former President had always been Calhoun's idol. He was from the South and Jackson was a Carolinian, so it was quite possible that Jefferson's name at the occasion might invoke some enthusiasm for his side. The third President had always maintained that the people were the only proper source of power. Basically, he was a nullifier, and Calhoun was quite hopeful.

The dining room at Embree's was appropriately decorated in the national colors, and the long table was gay with early spring flowers. President Jackson was seated at the head and Calhoun at the other end, the seats in between filled strictly according to protocol. All was serene. There was the usual confused hum of conversation; the steak was the best available, served in most generous quantity by suitably obsequious waiters. After the dessert dishes had been cleared away and the wine glasses filled, it was time for extempore toasts from each member of the party, ending, according to custom, with the President and Vice President. They were all, of course, laudatory of the first great democrat, vying with each other in attempts to show similarities between Jeffersonian democracy and the theories of Andrew Jackson—a hopeless effort in Calhoun's mind. As the last general toast was drunk, all eyes were turned towards "Old Hickory." There was a strange similarity between the two men at opposite ends of the table. Both were sharp-featured, both had white rather bristly hair and both sat tall in their chairs. There was, though, a subtle difference of expression. Calhoun's sharp features were somewhat softened by kindly, understanding eyes, while there was nothing in the President's eyes to discount the relentless sternness of his features.

Jackson rose to his full height and reached for his glass as the others followed suit. For a moment, he glanced down the table, bowing slightly to each side. Then, raising his glass, he looked directly down to his Vice President. Calhoun felt his hand trembling slightly as he lifted his glass from the table ready to respond to the President's toast, but he returned Jackson's stare with boldness. Then it came. In a voice that was almost a challenge, the toast was pronounced.

"Our Federal Union—it must be preserved." Calhoun drank to it. Then every eye was turned in his direction. The last two minutes had sealed his determination to hold fast to his convictions. He had not misinterpreted the President's look before he spoke, and his interpretation was proved by the toast that followed. He gladly took up the challenge. His voice was firm with an unmistakable determination.

"The Union—next to our liberty, the most dear."

The inference was clear. Glasses were raised. How much of the wine touched the President's lips would never be known. Chairs were pushed back. Jackson moved quickly away from the table and held a whispered conversation with his Secretary of State, Van Buren; the others broke up into groups. The waiters began quietly clearing the table. The guests left the hotel in twos and threes. Senator Hayne left with Calhoun. Not much was said as they strolled along Pennsylvania Avenue. At E Street, Hayne left him, and Calhoun walked home alone. A break with Jackson was inevitable.

~ VI ~

That night, Calhoun lay in bed staring into the darkness. Not even the occasional pressure of Floride's hand could smooth his jumbled thoughts. He knew now that he was on his own. He had friends, most loyal ones, but the vital decisions were his to make. As to his enemies, he was not quite sure. President Jackson had made his position as clear as though he had spelled it out.

If the difference in the toasts had been purely a matter of words, there would have been no reason for a quarrel, but Calhoun was well aware that to Jackson, the Union implied a centralized power. At the moment, he was in control, and to tolerate liberty was merely to weaken his own position. He had little conception of Calhoun's ideal Union, in which the minority had a voice that was not only heard but acted on. Could he any longer be numbered among his friends? Martin Van Buren, the Secretary of State, craved the succession and could hardly be called a friend. Crawford, his long-time friend and neigh-

bor in South Carolina, had long since shown his jealousy
of Calhoun's success, and Alexander Hamilton's son,
James, although still a supporter, had become increasingly cool over the past years. He was not the conniving
kind himself, but he was shrewd enough to recognize this
trait in others. The time was ripe for dirty politics. Jealousy, selfishness and personal enmity were rife in Washington, and he must follow decent principles. He was
right, but he had no idea just how dirty politics could be.
Little did he know that his two onetime friends had con-
spired to ruin him in his relations with Jackson, but he
was soon to find out.

A few days after the Jefferson dinner, Calhoun received
a letter from the President. This was not at all an unusual
occurrence, and he opened it most casually. It contained
a folded enclosure, and in the accompanying letter Jackson expressed great surprise at the statements presented
in the enclosure, "so different from what I had hitherto
believed to be correct." He asked for an explanation. Still
completely in the dark, Calhoun opened the enclosure.
It was a letter from William H. Crawford to Senator John
Forsyth asking the latter if his letter accusing Calhoun of
instigating the suggestion of a court-martial for Jackson
in the Seminole affair could be shown to the President.
Calhoun read it twice and then turned again to Jackson's
covering letter, "I desire," the President had written, "to
learn of you whether it be possible that the information
given is correct; whether it can be under all the circumstances of which you and I are both informed that any

attempt seriously to affect me was moved and sustained by you in the Cabinet council."

Coming on top of the implied threat of disagreement at the Jefferson dinner, this new issue struck him like an unexpected lightning bolt. It seemed to him almost like an insult to his personal honor and integrity. He must, of course, reply at once. He saw a break with Jackson, the end of his own Presidential ambition and, far more serious than this, his loss of influence in his defense of the Southern states and their rights as sovereign groups of people. This had become his life's work. Was it, he pondered, all to go for nothing? He sat quite still, struggling with these thoughts. Then he took up his pen and wrote to the President.

Yes, he wrote, the facts as implied in the enclosed letter were substantially correct. At the time of the Cabinet meeting referred to, he held the position of Secretary of War, and as such he had certain duties to perform which transcended all personal relationships. The discipline of the armed forces was vital and had to be maintained, and a general or another officer could not be given preferential treatment. Yes, he had made the official proposal for a court-martial, the matter had been freely discussed and the final decision in favor of General Jackson had been unanimous. He, as Secretary of War, had merely done his duty. He read and reread the letter and dispatched it to the White House. The immediate future was out of his hands.

The matter was obviously a plot to discredit him in

Jackson's eyes. Two names were mentioned in the letter, but he was shrewd enough to know the workings of a politician's mind, and other names occurred to him. Secretary of State Van Buren craved the Presidency, and he remembered how Jackson had held a whispered conversation with him at the end of the Jefferson dinner. Then, of course, there was James Hamilton, though this was hard to believe. Calhoun was convinced that he knew who the conspirators were. He convinced himself, though, that there was little use having any sort of personal quarrels with the possible exception of Van Buren. After all, he told himself, Crawford was too sick a man to have any serious presidential aspirations, and Hamilton was doing very well as governor of South Carolina. He preferred to keep the matter between the President and himself. Over the next few months, he had many talks with Jackson in which he tried most conscientiously to smooth out their relationship, and he felt that the irascible old general was cooling off somewhat. He couldn't help noticing, however, that the Secretary of State seemed to frequent the White House much more than his official duties could have required; but this thought could, of course, be merely a result of his own suspicions of Van Buren as one of the conspirators.

Peggy O'Neill, the wife of the Secretary of War, John H. Eaton, was attractive and popular, but she was originally a barmaid. Nothing could be said necessarily, against the morals of one in this profession, but the ladies of Washington assumed the worst, and they showed no hesitation in making their opinions quite clear. They snubbed her. They refused to call on her, and they were consistently out if she called on them; at dinners and balls, they ignored her. The President was in a most difficult position. He was a widower and not at all unsusceptible to feminine charm and, besides, Peggy was the wife of his Secretary of War and a break would be inconceivable. Calhoun had no particular personal feeling toward Peggy Eaton, but Floride Calhoun agreed with the other Washington ladies and, in spite of her husband's frequent urgings, refused to call on Peggy Eaton, who had already called on her. This in itself was perhaps her own business, but to General Jackson it verged on insult that the wife of his Vice President should refuse to meet the wife of his Secretary of War. It was difficult for him, but it was equally difficult for Calhoun. He loved his wife, and he most naturally went along with her except when protocol forced a brief meeting with the unpopular lady. He did his best to persuade Floride, but she was as stubborn as himself, and towards the end of 1831 she returned to her Southern plantation.

Calhoun soon realized that in spite of his generous attempts to improve relations with Jackson, the Exposition disclosures, the Seminole matter, the Peggy Eaton affair and, of course, some prodding from Van Buren had convinced the President that a break was essential. Soon private whispering became public talk. Jackson himself spoke openly of Calhoun as "an ambitious demagogue," a remark that came with curious inconsistency from a man who gloried in his personal power. Calhoun expressed his own opinion of Jackson to a friend as "that upstart martinet in the White House." It was not easy for Calhoun to accept this new state of affairs. Had not Jackson been the hero of the War of 1812, which he himself had fostered and which he thought lost until the old general won the victory at New Orleans?

In order to explain his court-martial proposal of 1819 to the public, Calhoun decided to write out a statement. He still felt that his procedure at the time had been purely routine with no personal overtones, and that the country had a right to know that certain members of the government had seen fit to distort the facts for their own political advancement, and to disparage him in the eyes of the President. He hesitated a little, thinking that perhaps it would be too impolitic, and did submit the manuscript through a friend to the Secretary of War, Eaton. Apparently there was some faint desire on the part of the President to patch up their differences because, with a few minor changes, the statement was approved. On February 22, 1831, it appeared in the *U.S. Telegraph.*

Ever since the "Tariff of Abominations," the Southern states had begun to grow more and more disturbed. Their feelings about the new tariff ranged from mild protests to most violent demands. The former were universal, but the latter were limited to a few states, of which South Carolina was the leader. Calhoun summed up his personal view of the situation to his friend Duff Green, editor of the Washington *Telegraph.* He pointed out that the tariff bill was un-Constitutional and a threat both to the fundamental rights of the South and the preservation of the Union. He was fearful, though, that the extremists in his home state might turn to violence, and he felt deeply that such violence would have tragic results.

When he reached his home, Fort Hill, he held a meeting with leaders of the state and discussed the whole problem. He said he saw only two alternatives: to go along with Jackson in the hope that he could be persuaded to reduce the tariff in order to relieve the suffering the high rates inflicted on the South or accept the extreme measure of veto or interposition of the states. He avoided the word "nullification," which was in common use. Of the two choices, he definitely favored the first. In his heart he had little faith that Jackson could be persuaded, but he took his stand in the hope of postponing a too radical move on the part of his state.

He hesitated to press the theory of nullification too far, although, logically, he felt sure it was the right of a sovereign state, lest more tragic consequences might result. Actual secession was uppermost in his mind, but he couldn't help hearing from various parts of the country unmistakable whisperings against the South's "peculiar institution" of slavery. It was possible, he thought to himself, that a bill to abolish slavery might be passed, and no matter how hard he tried to push it aside, the thought kept recurring that the real issue was slavery and not the high tariff. Its abolition would be a death blow to the

South. Not only was Negro labor a *sine qua non* in the intense heat of the cotton and corn fields, but generations had been brought up to accept a mode of life which abolition of slavery would utterly destroy. It was a grim picture that he conjured up, but one not easily erased, and if nullification should be pressed too hard, it might become a reality.

He had another reason for not wanting to declare himself for nullification too strongly. Timothy Dwight's casual remark of almost forty years before had become more than casual over the years, and although his hopes were dimming, they still preyed on his mind. If he announced himself as a nullifier, he would lose the vote of the North. He made no definitive public statement, but he did confide in his friend J. H. Hammond that he felt Jackson had reneged on all his political promises and was losing control of the Republican Party, and that he himself had much strength throughout the country, especially in Kentucky, Tennessee, Pennsylvania and his own home state. He knew perfectly well that the charge of cheap political ambition had already been leveled against him, but then, he knew this was the staple argument of political enemies. In all honesty, he could not deny some personal ambitions to the Presidency, but that was not his sole motive. He did not feel that Union and states' rights were inconsistent conceptions. Strict majority rule, he felt, was inconsistent with states' rights, and he had coined the phrase "concurrent majority" to express his idea. North,

South and West must in some way be reconciled. At present, the North was, through its protectionist policy, dominating the South, and this must be stopped if the Union were to survive. As President, he would have a chance of seeing his theories realized.

His hesitation to commit himself was somewhat frustrated by an influence beyond his control. On May 19, 1831, George MacDuffie, a representative from upstate South Carolina and Calhoun's right-hand man, was given a dinner in Charleston. Toasts were drunk to nullification, and MacDuffie delivered a belligerent, though eloquent speech in favor of it. He ended with these words: "Shall we be terrified by mere phantoms of blood when our ancestors for less cause encountered the reality? . . . The idea of bloodshed and civil war in a contest of this kind is utterly ridiculous. . . ." Silence and apparent indifference were now impossible, and on August 3, 1831, Calhoun frankly announced his position on the vital issue in a letter to the Pendleton *Messenger*.

His hand had been forced. He was now a "nullifier." To be sure, his authorship of the recent "Exposition and Protest of the South Carolina Legislature" had been widely known for a year, but the statements in it were protests against Northern infringements of the rights of sovereign states and not solutions for the problem. Calhoun had always disliked the word "nullification" and endeavored to avoid it in general conversation. Unfortunately, his supporters—MacDuffie and young Hamilton —were known to be ardently in favor of this drastic procedure, and the public did not hesitate to link him with them.

Early in 1832, Congress passed a new tariff bill meant, Calhoun supposed, as a sop to the South. The changes, however, were so inconsequential that the situation was practically unaltered. Furthermore, Congress at the same time passed a bill to renew the charter of the Bank of the United States, which was not to expire for two years. This latter was vetoed by Jackson because, he said, he was an enemy of monopoly, and the bank was merely a method of taking from the poor to give to the rich. This was most disappointing to Calhoun, who had consistently favored a national bank ever since the chaotic days following the War of 1812, when the country's finances were in a deplorable state. The passing of the futile tariff bill and the vetoing of one in which he believed not only increased his feelings of hopelessness but made him feel that nullification wasn't such a bad idea after all.

The "little martinet in the White House," as Calhoun called him, was in quite a different state of mind. His protectionist policy had given him New York's forty-four electoral votes, and he had decided to run again. He was feeling his power, and his age and infirmity were forgotten, as was his tacit understanding with Calhoun. After the adjournment of the Twenty-Second Congress in April 1832, he took a rather dramatic step. He asked for the resignation of those Cabinet members who were loyal to Calhoun. These included the Secretary of the Treasury, the Secretary of the Navy and the Attorney-General.

These men were replaced by strong protectionists, such as Louis McLane of Delaware, Edward Livingston and Roger Taney.

The writing on the wall indicated clearly to Calhoun that Jackson would be elected to a second term and that Van Buren would succeed him, but he refused to give in entirely. His constant defense of the rights of the Southern states gave him a strong following in that section, and on his way home from Washington after the adjournment of the Twenty-Second Congress he did considerable electioneering, conferring with party leaders and speaking at various dinners. He read where Clay had said "Calhoun is a dead duck politically," but it didn't disturb him. He had become hardened to political jealousy and bitterness, even from an old friend.

One thing was becoming very clear to him. His position as Vice President made it wholly impossible for him to express his sentiments as clearly as he would like, and the difficulty was intensified by the forced resignation of his friends in the Cabinet. Furthermore, under the new circumstances, it could not possibly lead to his succession to the Presidency. He must, he concluded, rely now wholly on his popularity in the country. From the middle of 1832, he deliberately absented himself from the Senate.

Two things now militated against him. There was no doubt that Jackson's hatred of him would be reflected in executive actions, and his now open position as a nullifier brought opposition, though not always hatred, from the Unionists of the South. This latter fact was a bitter pill

for him to swallow, as he felt that he was as good a
Unionist as any man alive. The Unionist sentiment was
widespread except in South Carolina. Meetings and dinners were held, resolutions were passed and violence occasionally flared up. In Spartanburg, North Carolina,
effigies of Calhoun and young Hamilton were hung in
the public square.

The Unionist sentiment was conservative. They agreed
in essence with Calhoun and his friends, but they clung
to the hope that somehow the tariff might be reduced.
They accepted even the unsatisfactory changes in Clay's
new bill which stirred the nullifiers to action, relying on
Jackson's frequent public assurances that some reforms
would soon be made. Their position was a fairly strong
one, and Calhoun's nullification theories were held in
check. After months of inaction, however, it became increasingly evident that, in spite of Jackson's protestations,
permanency rather than reform was the purpose of the
administration. Calhoun's party grew in numbers and
strength.

In his own mind, Calhoun had consistently defined
nullification as "such an interposition of state sovereignty
as may be effectual for the preservation of states' rights."

He had said many times, "I believe the cause to be the
cause of truth and justice, of Union, liberty and the Constitution."

As the Unionists began to capitulate, he feared that his
definition of nullification might be distorted by hotheads
and result in some tragic occurrence. He had not long to

wait before finding out just how far his fears were justified. Towards the end of 1832, a state election showed the nullifiers definitely in the majority in spite of considerable physical violence on the part of the Unionists. Calhoun noted especially that the old antagonism between the up-country and the Charleston areas that had existed when he was a boy had eased. Misfortune had united them. With this favorable start, Calhoun wrote to a friend that the next step would be the calling of a State Convention and the nullifying of the obnoxious act. Everything would be done, he assured his correspondent, with a view to preserving the Union. He never let this thought be forgotten in spite of the prevalence of secessionist talk among more radical thinkers.

On November 24, 1832, the Convention was called. Those opposed to nullification were in a very definite minority. One correspondent wrote that "the death knell of submission has been sounded." Still fearful of overly radical moves, Calhoun wrote an open letter to Massachusetts outlining the purpose of the Convention and stressing his earnest desire for a peaceful solution to the problem. He clung to this hope, but the Convention's final "Ordinance of Nullification" was very violent. It at least cleared the air, declaring unequivocally in the name of the sovereign people of South Carolina that the Acts of 1828 and 1832 were un-Constitutional. It went on to declare the acts "null and void, and no law, not binding upon the state, its officers or citizens." It defied the federal government to collect any customs duties within the state after February 1, 1833, and went so far as to threaten instant secession if the government attempted to use force. Calhoun regretted the challenging language and waited nervously for the reaction from Washington. He didn't have long to wait. Within two weeks Jackson sent reinforcements to the two forts in Charleston Harbor and revenue cutters to the port to force collection of duties. The ardent Unionists in South Carolina were, of course, overjoyed, and they cooperated in every way with the President.

The city of Charleston was a seething cauldron of protest. Notwithstanding Calhoun's popularity and his incessant pleas for patience and moderation, disunion sentiment was the order of the day. It became fashionable to give dinners and balls and form clubs to encourage hesitant citizens. Fiery articles appeared in many papers, and a "Disunion Drama" was produced at the theater.

In the midst of all this turmoil, Senator Haynes, one of Calhoun's warmest supporters, was elected governor of South Carolina to succeed young James Hamilton. This left an empty seat in the Senate, and to South Carolinians the natural choice to fill out the unexpired term was John C. Calhoun, the popular "defender of South Carolina." Calhoun was naturally pleased, as it gave him a chance to plead the case of the South before the nation's legislature, but he had personal thoughts that he kept to himself. He had started his national polical career in the Senate, and had very nearly realized his private dream. Perhaps with this new start the dream would become a reality. After all, he was only fifty. He was still technically Vice President, although he had absented himself from Washington since July. His place as President of the Senate had been taken by Hugh L. White, "the Vice President of the United States being absent." A few days after Christmas, he sent his formal notice of resignation to the Secretary of State. He transmitted it to the President, who was undoubtedly delighted.

Dec. 10 1832

Cal., So. Car. 28 Dec. 1832

Sir:

Having concluded to accept of a seat in the Senate to which I have been elected by the legislature of this state, I herewith resign the office of Vice Pres. of the U.S.

Very respectfully
Your ob ser &
J. C. Calhoun

Hon. H. Livingston
Sec. of State

∽ VII ∽

The President may have been delighted, but it was not at all the usual thing for a Vice President to resign, and the consequences were any man's guess. To be sure, Calhoun was back in the Senate—not only an honor in itself but the national forum before which to plead the cause of his beloved South Carolina. On the other hand, he knew quite well the quality of the opposition he would have to face. His political enemy and brother War Hawk of 1812, Henry Clay, with his often vicious sarcasm, and Daniel Webster, skilled in oratory and merciless to an opponent in debate, were dangerous adversaries. As President of the Senate under Adams and Jackson, he had been able to merely keep order and break ties by casting his vote. For years, he had not addressed so large and important a body, and he feared that lack of practice might well have dulled the edge of his usually sharp reasoning. Logic, he was well aware, was not the only weapon to be used against him. Personal hatred, jealousy

and selfishness would motivate many of the arguments.
Those representing manufacturing states, abolitionists
and strong nationalists each had his own particular ax
to grind. It was not a promising picture, and at the end
of December, he left for Washington with very mixed
emotions, his absolute belief in his cause giving him the
strength to carry on.

While he braced himself to face difficult political problems, he was often faced with personal ones not always
easy to stand up to. His favorite son, Andrew, who had
never been much of a scholar, had been persuaded to
enter Yale and for a year or two had shown great promise.
Then a most unexpected and rather unusual situation
arose. The college instituted a required course on the
subject of "conic sections," covering such conceptions as
ellipse, parabola and hyperbola. To many of the students,
and Andrew Calhoun was one of them, an abstract subject like this was utterly useless and a complete waste of
time. They protested, and when this did not produce any
result, they left the university. Shortly after, many of
them returned, but not Andrew. This was a great disappointment to Calhoun, although he could not help agree-
ing with the protesters. Such national problems as tariff
and disunion made a study of "conic sections" seem to
him utterly ridiculous.

There was tenseness in the capital city as the day for
the opening of the Twenty-Third Session approached.
Calhoun had even been warned that he would be arrested

when he reached Washington, although he found it difficult to imagine the charge. He had been called a "dead
duck" politically, and he had been hanged in effigy in
Spartanburg; but his years in politics had taught him
that in a political war there would always be more bark-
ing than biting.

It had been a bitterly cold winter and the Potomac was
frozen over, so he made the trip overland. The last year
had been a difficult and tiring one, and he had looked
forward to a brief rest on the packet boat. But nature
forced him to use the rough, circuitous roads. He arrived
in Washington on January 4 and took a room at Gadsby's,
going to bed early in preparation for the difficult days
ahead. The next morning, he rode to the Capitol in a cab
over streets so icy that the driver had difficulty keeping
his horse from falling. To Calhoun's surprise, Pennsylvania Avenue was lined with people, but whether the
turnout was for a conquering hero or a condemned crim-
inal there was no way of telling. It was just a mass of
staring faces and, try as he might, it was impossible to
tell friend from foe.

At the Capitol, he took the seat vacated by Hayne. He
was conscious of a tenseness in the Senate Chamber, and
the gallery was packed with another sea of silent, stony
faces. Members in front turned as he sat down, and he
almost felt the staring eyes of those behind him. He tried
to feel philosophical about it, but it was a difficult situation. He knew very well what the business of this first

session was. The so-called Force Bill, called by its opponents "The Bloody Bill," was to be presented and discussed, and Clay was to offer his compromise tariff bill. Calhoun was unalterably opposed to the "Force Bill," which would authorize the government to use whatever means might be necessary to compel payment of duties in the South. As to Clay's Compromise, he was waiting to make up his mind on that vital subject. In the meantime, he had prepared three resolutions, stating the position of the South in the crisis. If his resolutions came up for a vote and were favorably dealt with, the "Force Bill" would be automatically disposed of. This, however, turned out to be wishful thinking. Immediately after the "Force Bill" was introduced, Calhoun rose to present his resolutions.

Before he did so, he felt compelled to reply to Senator Wilkins of Pennsylvania, who had stated categorically that South Carolina intended to use force to break the law.

"I cannot sit silent," he said, "and permit such erroneous constructions to go forth. South Carolina has never contemplated violent resistance to the laws of the United States." Then, looking straight at Senator Wilkins, he repeated a statement that the Senator had sneeringly quoted. "The day when the discussion of the Force Bill takes place will present a crisis more solemn and important than the Declaration of Independence." Then he proceeded to offer his resolutions. He said he had drawn them with great care.

Though the Force Bill is ostensibly applicable to all states, it is obviously aimed at South Carolina with the intention not of putting down the lawless combinations of individuals in that state, but the authorized opposition of South Carolina to an act which she conscientiously believes un-Constitutional and oppressive and, as such, exercising the right which belongs to her in the last resort as a sovereign member of the confederacy, she has declared null and void. This poses the awfully important question —Has Congress the right to pass this bill?

The President claims that the people of these United States are united on the principle of a social compact. The Constitution itself says, "The Constitution is binding upon the States ratifying the same." What could be more explicit? Sovereignty lies with the States and not the government. It lies in the people of twenty-four states as forming distinct political communities confederated in this Union. . . . But two modes of political existence cannot long endure in our country. The one that was formed, by the framers of our admirable constitution, a federal system uniting free and independent states in a bond of union for mutual advantages and to be preserved by the concurrent assent of the parts—or a government of the sword. The choice is before us.

"For what purpose," he asked, "is the unlimited control of the purse and of the sword placed at the disposition of the Executive?" The law had been, he said, used throughout history by tyrants for the torturing of individuals and the extinction of races. He spoke to hushed galleries. In spite of his depleted energy, his voice was strong and his logic was undeniable. The Senate, however, refused to accept his premise, going only so far as to assure him that South Carolina's reasoning would be attached to the Presidential proclamation when the bill came up for debate. Calhoun would have to bide his time, and a debate with Daniel Webster, the obvious spokesman for the government, loomed ahead of him.

Before this could take place, a vote was taken on Clay's compromise tariff. Calhoun listened intently to Clay's suggestions of gradual reduction of duties to a point that would satisfy South Carolina without the use of the "Force Bill." They were honeyed words that he heard, and it seemed to him that the plan would at least prevent an immediate disruption of the Union. He rose in turn and voted in favor of the compromise. It was not what had been expected, and the galleries responded with tumultuous applause. So great was it and so interspersed with cries of approval that the chairman ordered the galleries cleared, and only with difficulty was persuaded to change his order to a warning. Clay and Calhoun in agreement! What next? Actually, the two men, although quite different in temperament, were united in one respect. They both wanted to preserve the Union even though their premises were far apart. Calhoun would, perhaps, have been willing to shake hands. But Clay never ceased to dislike Calhoun.

In spite of the surprise it caused, Calhoun felt that his vote was logical on the assumption that the South Carolina legislature would repeal the disputed Ordinance of Nullification. If they didn't, the "Force Bill" would go into effect, and Northern troops would be sent into his home state with results that were too terrible to imagine. He must get his resolutions before the Senate, hoping to get a favorable vote. It would be a last stand against an inexorable enemy. The question was put and was opened by the chairman for debate from the floor. The expectant silence showed clearly how eagerly the Senate, whatever each member's views might be, craved a solution to the problem. They knew well that the main debate would be between Calhoun and Webster, two top actors in the drama. The curtain was up, but neither star spoke. It was obvious that each was waiting for the other, hoping for the stronger position in the argument. Across the aisle, Calhoun watched Webster, who sat with folded hands and unseeing eyes. There was no sign of movement, and reluctantly Calhoun rose to speak. He had determined to avoid much reference to his own resolutions, as he was sure that Webster would aim his guns in that direction and he hoped to confuse his opponent by a different approach. As the galleries watched in silence, he moved the chairs from behind the long table at the end of the room. He needed space to move as he spoke. He knew he had

friends among the crowd that stared at him, but he also
knew that there were those who for political or personal
reasons were ready to condemn him regardless of what he
might say.

> The real question at issue is, has the government
> a right to impose burdens on the capital and indus-
> try of one portion of the country, not with a view to
> revenue, but to benefit another? . . . If gentlemen
> suppose that the stand taken by the people of Caro-
> lina rests on passion and delusion, they are wholly
> mistaken. The case is far otherwise. No community
> from the legislator to the ploughman were ever bet-
> ter instructed in their rights, and the resistance on
> which the State has resolved is the result of mature
> reflection. . . .

He pointed out the injustice of the charge that both
he and his state were the authors of the protective system
on the ground that they had supported the tariff of 1816.
At that date, he told them, the country was in most severe
financial straits, and the tariff which at that time he defended had as its objective the raising of revenue and
only incidentally the giving of protection.

"South Carolina's objection," he continued, "is not
against the improper modification of a bill acknowledged
to be for revenue, but that under the name of imposts, a
power essentially different from the taxing power is ex-

ercised, partaking much more of the character of a penalty than a tax. . . ."

He defended himself against the charge of personal ambition and chided Webster for bringing personalities into a discussion so vital to the existence of the Union. "Whatever may have been the intent of the Senator, I assure him I will not follow his example. I never had any inclination to gladiatorial exhibitions in the halls of legislation." By Saturday, he had been speaking for six hours. He thanked the Senate for their indulgence and took his seat prepared to listen to Webster's reply. The Pennsylvania orator spoke until eight o'clock in the evening. It was bitterly cold and snowing outside, which perhaps drove many into the shelter of the Senate chamber, but Webster was always a drawing card and Northern sentiment was eager for a victory over the "nullifier."

"Calhoun's cause," Webster opened by saying, "finds no basis in the Constitution; no succor from public sympathy, no cheering from a patriotic community. He is like a strong man struggling in a morass." He found his idea of American liberty far different from Calhoun's and objected to the use of the phrase "Constitutional compact," in spite of the fact that he had used the same expression in a speech in 1830. He claimed that sovereignty was "something from across the sea" and had no legitimate place in the government of the United States. He quite disregarded Calhoun's theory of "concurrent majority," holding fast with de Tocqueville that government should be based on the greatest good for the greatest number.

The right of state interposition, a phrase Calhoun preferred to "nullification," he said, "strikes at the very foun-
dation of the legislative power of Congress." He spent
much time on the strict meanings of words used by Calhoun, such as "accede," "secede" and "compact." There
was no mention of the legitimate protest against the unfairness of the tariff so clearly evidenced by the universal
wearing in South Carolina of the blue cockade and Pal-
metto button as a sign of justifiable protest. Congress had
spoken and must be obeyed, a view that to Calhoun appeared only a subtle and false argument.

Weeks of heated debates, resolutions and amendments
had gone by. The press and the public had a prolonged
field day. Calhoun had fought logically, fluently and,
above all, sincerely for the cause of justice as he saw it.
Webster, the somewhat reluctant voice of the central government, had backed Andrew Jackson with his usual dramatic oratory.

Towards the end of February, the "Force Bill" and
Clay's Compromise Tariff were passed by a substantial
vote.

Calhoun was tired. It was a mental as well as a physical
weariness which the vote only partially relieved. The nullification stand of South Carolina had indeed brought
about immediate reduction in the obnoxious duties and
a promise of further concessions; but the Force Bill had
been passed and was on the statute books as a threat to
the states' rights doctrine. The South Carolina legislature

had authorized a second state convention to assemble on March 13 to consider the possibility of secession. Would his partial victory in Congress in any way appease the hotheads in South Carolina? If he were there, Calhoun felt fairly sure, he could persuade them to a moderate course, but it was already March 4 and the convention at Columbia was only eight days away. The distance to be covered was four hundred miles, the winter was especially severe and the roads, in a questionable state in the best of times, would be almost impassable. His first choice would have been the packet boat, but the Potomac was still partly frozen over, and he had no alternative but the overland route.

He started from Washington in the regular stage; but the heavy vehicle proved inconceivably slow, and at Alexandria he climbed into an open mail cart. It was bitterly cold and the coarse heavily padlocked mail sacks hardly afforded the minimum of comfort, but Calhoun was desperate. Should the convention choose to nullify the new tariff bill, the consequences could not help but be tragic. He must get to Columbia in time to make a last stand for rational thinking. The Union was threatened, and although he himself was now avowedly a states' rights advocate, the fundamental Union had to be preserved.

Huddled among the sacks, he had plenty of hours for thinking. Sleep was a matter of brief half-hours, broken each time the cart dropped into a hole or gave a sudden jolt when a plank in the road had rotted away. The frequent changes of horses gave him welcome chances to

stretch, but most of the time he spent in irregular naps
and a frank summing up of his own position in the crisis.
Andrew Jackson represented to him the growing tend-
ency towards usurpation of all power by the central government. He had been criticized as a nullifier, which his
detractors said was merely another word for secessionist,
but he had never meant it that way. To him, nullification
was a negative power—that of preventing or arresting the
action of the government. It might be called by a number of names—veto, interposition, nullification, check or
balance of power. He had coined the term "concurrent
majority," by which the wishes and welfare of an honest
minority might be protected. In the dreariness of his present helpless position, he felt that he was justified in his
stand. After all, to render a unanimous decision, a jury
must compromise. He couldn't help thinking back to the
legislation on voting when he had joined the South Carolina Legislature twenty-six years before. The rights of his
upland compatriots had then been recognized by a rea-
sonable compromise.

He found himself falling into somewhat confused philosophical thoughts—mesmerized, perhaps, by the black
sky and the mass of stars that moved irregularly from side
to side at every lurch of the springless cart. He disagreed
with the social contract theory that man is good by nature. Man's natural state is social and political, he thought,
and because man is fundamentally selfish, he must be
controlled. Philosophy became confused with his per-

sonal problems, and he dozed off into a deep sleep that even the cold and the plank roads could not disturb.

He was awakened at Columbia. The convention had been in session for a day and, fearful lest he was too late, he hurried to the convention hall in his crumpled coat and muddy boots. He was greeted by friends and given a seat, but there was much whispering, not only about his weary, haggard and unkempt appearance and bloodshot and sunken eyes, but also about his vote for the tariff bill. News of this had left Washington before Calhoun. The hotheads deplored it as a faithless move against South Carolina. Calhoun knew perfectly well what was in their minds and, rather than try to make a speech in his enfeebled condition, he moved quietly from one member to another, pointing out to each that South Carolina had won a distinct victory. The threat of nullification had resulted in a substantial degree of capitulation on the part of the government, and to carry the dispute further would only open the flood gates of actual war. He had the assistance, strangely enough, of Benjamin Leigh of Virginia, who was present as a mediator between South Carolina and the United States. Virginia disapproved of the principle of nullification, although she was in sympathy with the general protest against the high duties. They did, however, nullify the "Force Bill," although one member asked quite pointedly how they expected to nullify the United States Army.

Calhoun had won a victory, but he was soon to find

that it was merely the momentary damming up of an ir-resistable flood of events that would occupy his energies and time for the rest of his life.

In 1831, William Lloyd Garrison, a printer by trade and a violent reformer by vocation, had established a Boston newspaper, *The Liberator,* dedicated to "the im-mediate and unconditional emancipation" of all slaves. In 1833 the American Anti-Slavery Society was formed, unequivocally declaring war on the system of slavery. Calhoun had feared this for years, but for a time he con-tented himself with sarcastic references to the "fanatics and madmen of the North." He had other problems. In 1836, President Jackson, fearing the growing power of Nathaniel Biddle's United States Bank, planned to re-move all the government deposits from it and distribute them among the state banks. In order to do this, he dis-missed two secretaries of the treasury who disagreed with him, and finally appointed Roger B. Taney, who went along with the idea. To Calhoun this appeared most au-tocratic, and it increased his fears that the government was turning into a one-man affair. Shortly after the de-posits were removed with the permission of newly ap-pointed Secretary Taney, Calhoun voiced a protest, di-rected particularly to Roger Taney. "Can he," asked Cal-houn, "be ignorant of the fact that the whole power of the government has been perverted into a great political machine, with a view to corrupting and controlling the country?" He was criticized even by many of his friends because he had advocated the United States Bank in the

first place. In fact, it had been called his bank. His reply
was, as usual, logical and true. He had been in favor of a
central bank in 1816 because the economy of the country
following the war was a shambles. The mismanagement
that followed was not in the least his responsibility. One
must, he insisted, divorce the government and the banking system.

No sooner had Jackson withdrawn the deposits than
Biddle ordered the "Monster of Chestnut Street" to cur-
tail all loans. With no money in the crop-moving season
in the South and West, there was a flood of business fail-
ures. Men were put out of work, and panic struck. Webster and Clay urged Biddle to restore the loans, but the
damage was done. In 1836 the "Monster" closed its doors.
Calhoun's contention that the proper method was a state-
chartered bank was adopted by New York in 1838, and
the system spread over the country.

Calhoun was disturbed by a number of other things
in the national picture; and more and more he felt that
his was a voice crying in the wilderness. The encroachments, under Jackson, of the rights of the states, the emphasis in the North on business and profits and the utter
disregard of a whole section of the country and, of late,
the whisperings of abolitionism were all issues on which
he felt deeply. He did not feel that either party, Whig or
Democratic, presented any valid answer. Shortly after
his partial victory at the Nullification Convention, he expressed his feelings about partisanship.

"I stand wholly disconnected with the two great parties now contending for ascendency. My political connections are with that small and denounced party which has voluntarily retired from the party strife of the day, with a view of saving, if possible, the liberty and the Constitution of the country in this great crisis of our affairs." His stand became known as Calhounism and marked him as a "loner." All through the South, he was tendered banquets for his stand against the government; he politely but firmly refused. He had often been accused of personal ambition, but though he often yearned for the Presidency, his fundamental desire for a union of friendly states, as envisioned by its founders, was his primary goal. In reply to one invitation to a public dinner, he politely regretted, and added a statement of his personal feelings.

"I utter it," he wrote, "under a painful but solemn conviction that we are no longer a free people, a people living under a Constitution, as the guardian of their rights; but under the absolute rule of an unchecked majority which has usurped the power to do as it pleases and to enforce its pleasure at the point of the bayonet. . . ."

As had been expected, Jackson's nominee, Martin Van Buren, was elected President in 1837. He inherited the worst financial panic that the United States had known up to that time. Banks almost universally closed their doors, cotton and tobacco and other staples became worthless and desperate men walked the streets looking for work. Their desperation led to the looting of banks and strongboxes. Securities had no value, and counterfeit money was flooding the country. Calhoun had no friendly feelings for Van Buren. He had managed Jackson's campaign and had been practically nominated as his successor. He could hardly be expected to show undue enthusiasm over the little man from Kinderhook. Nevertheless, he supported him—partly, his conscience freely admitted, as a political maneuverer and partly because of his stand on the banking issue. The new President publicly expressed the thought that Calhoun had urged for some time—that government and banking should be divorced—even conceiving the idea of an independent Government Treasury with branches in the states and no connection with any commercial bank. The idea, Calhoun felt, was sound, and it was put into effect—only to be repealed under the Tyler administration. The bank question severely divided the politicians and brought about violent and often malicious oratory in Congress, but there was another issue in which Calhoun played a more prominent part and which not only divided the politicians but threatened the very existence of the Union. This issue was the "peculiar institution" that was the life blood of the South—slavery.

~ VIII ~

All through the years of his enthusiasm for nationalism, his belief in the unity of the country and his desire to encourage the industry of the Northern states, as evidenced by his support in 1816 of some form of protection, Calhoun had belittled the idea that the South's "peculiar institution" of slavery could possibly bring about disunion. It appeared to him as normal as the existing class of laborers in the manufacturing plants of the North. As Secretary of War under Monroe (1817–25), he worked tirelessly for more efficiency in armed forces as an essential factor in holding together the rapidly increasing pieces of the United States "jig-saw." During his three years as Vice President, the theory of Negro slavery was one of the least of his problems.

Then John Quincy Adams, the son of the second president, conceived and put into effect the Tariff of 1828, the "Tariff of Abominations." Calhoun had taken up the gauntlet for the South. Slavery was not then an im-

120

mediate issue. The threat of disunion had risen over the tariff.

But there had been incidents that, like the ripples on the surface of a quiet sea, presaged a coming storm. As far back as 1791, there was a Negro uprising in Santo Domingo led by an ex-slave named Toussaint L'Ouverture, who had died later in a French dungeon. In 1807, sentiment against slavery rose in England—at first admittedly more on economic grounds than humanitarian. In 1833, slavery was abolished in all English possessions. The South American countries, when freed from Spain, followed suit. The Missouri Compromise of 1820 raised the ripples of warning to waves of threat that were not in the least stilled by the fugitive slave laws. South Carolina, Virginia and Mississippi suffered bloody revolts. William Lloyd Garrison began publishing his antislavery paper in 1831, and two years later the American Anti-Slavery Society was formed.

In the South, slavery was an integral part of the whole plantation system. Stimulated by Eli Whitney's 1793 invention of the cotton gin for separating the seeds from the fiber, it became vital to the region's existence. Southerners, in the wake of the bloody slave insurrections and the growing Northern abolition sentiment, were terrified. In spite of his optimistic denials of any danger to the Union from antislavery propaganda, Calhoun found himself in a dilemma. As a Southerner and a planter, he well understood the absolute necessity of slave labor until some substitute could be found. On the other hand, his dream of a strong Union had never dissipated. He would have it ruled on the principle of "concurrent majority" in which the wishes of the minority would receive equal attention, rather than the biased government he was beginning to fear, but a Union nevertheless. He had once called the abolitionists "fanatics," but with the increase of their propaganda, distributed largely among the slaves, he had to admit that there was an ominous cleavage growing between two sections of the country.

By 1836, petitions were being circulated to abolish slavery in the District of Columbia. In January of that year, Calhoun took a bold step. He offered a motion in the Senate not to receive the petitions for serious consideration. It was a bold step and one not calculated to appeal to many Southerners. He was instantly criticized on the ground that by raising the issue publicly in Congress, he was playing into the hands of the abolitionists. Slavery, his critics pointed out, was definitely authorized by the Constitution, an authorization that could be changed only by an amendment against which the entire South would vote. Calhoun had never been afraid of opposing even his friends when he felt that an underlying principle was at stake, and he answered his friendly critics characteristically.

He had always been, he reminded them, a patriotic defender of the Union and a loyal son of South Carolina. In this case, he felt it a duty both to the Union and to the Southern states to speak against a bill which, if enacted into law, would without question split the Union in two.

This time he seemed to possess a crystal ball, and what he saw in it he was not in the least afraid to describe. Furthermore, he pointed out, one cannot condemn a system of any kind in one part of the Union without implying that it should receive the same treatment in another. "The petitions were," he said, ". . . a foul slander on nearly one-half of the states of the Union." He accepted his critics' reminder that slavery was recognized by the Constitution and asked them pointedly if the petitions were allowed, would not the petitioners be violating the spirit of the Constitution. Article one of the amendments, he admitted, says that "Congress shall make no law prohibiting the people to petition the government for a redress of their grievances." There is, however, he noted, no clause compelling Congress to receive the petitions. If all petitions of any kind on every subject should be received and considered by Congress, the Legislature not only would be swamped in a tidal wave of paper but might easily have to consider such a petition as one to outlaw God. To back up this view, he quoted one of his idols, Thomas Jefferson, who had contended that the contents of any petition must be carefully noted and a vote taken whether to accept or reject.

The discussion continued for four months. The Senate was relatively dignified, but violence nearly exploded in the House. Technicalities, prejudices, falsehoods and political ambitions often clouded the issue, but Calhoun was on his feet constantly to bring the matter to a head. He was glad of the opportunity to meet the issue face to

face. He had known as far back as 1820 that a confronta-
tion was inevitable, although he had tried to belittle the
possibilities. At that time, he had said that he could
scarcely conceive of a cause of sufficient power to divide
the Union except a victory of the abolitionists. Then he
added, "Should so dangerous a mode of believing once
take root, no one can calculate the consequences." In his
heart, he felt that he was championing an already lost
cause, but he refused to raise the white flag. He defended
slavery in the South. He admitted the cruelties of ignorant overseers; he abhorred, he said, the Northern states'
traffic in slaves, which no honest Northerner would dare
deny. He held that "there never has yet existed a wealthy
and civilized society in which one portion of the community did not, in point of fact, live on the labor of the
other. To accomplish this end there are almost innum-
erable devices from the brute force and gross superstition
of ancient times to the subtle and artful fiscal contri-
vances of modern. . . ." As he spoke, he had in mind
small children working in Northern textile mills and half-
naked women dragging coal carts in dismal mines, but he
knew his listeners would also have this vision, and it was
not his habit to emphasize the obvious. "I might," he continued, "well challenge a comparison between them and
the more direct, simple and patriarchal mode by which
the labor of the African race is, among us, commanded
by the European. I may say with truth that in few countries is so much left to the share of the laborer, and so
little exacted from him or where there is more kind at-

tention paid to him in sickness or in infirmities of age. . . . Emancipation would not satisfy these fanatics. . . . The next step would be to raise the Negroes to a social and political equality with the whites and, that being effected, we would soon see the present condition of the two races reversed."

These months of bickering resulted finally in a partial victory for Calhoun. Congress went on record as holding "that domestic slavery . . . composes an important part certain states' domestic institutions inherited from their ancestors and existing at the adoption of the Constitution . . . and that no change of opinion . . . on the part of the other states of the Union . . . can justify them in open . . . attacks thereon with a view to its overthrow."

Calhoun naturally was pleased, but he intuitively knew that this was but a respite. He had said many times that the question of abolition "was the only question of sufficient magnitude . . . to divide this Union and divide it, it would, or drench the country in blood, if not arrested." He was also enough of a political veteran to know that much of the Northerners' acquiescence in the point of view of the South was due to a fear of losing it not only as a source of votes but as a good customer for Northern products.

The Twenty-Fourth Congress dealt with many issues besides slavery, and Calhoun was by no means silent on any of them. He had always made a point of carefully studying all issues, and once he had reached a conclusion he rarely abandoned it. Jackson advocated a declaration

of war over the money which France owed the United
States. Calhoun opposed his attitude, saying that the
course the President was taking was hasty and would
force the United States into a hopeless war for a most
trivial cause. His point was well taken, and the matter
was soon forgotten. He had stood almost alone in opposition to the President, and his view had been proved
correct.

A movement had been started by Senator Benton of
Missouri to permit the expunging of certain articles from
the official records. Calhoun saw the possibility that resolutions made in favor of the slaveholding states might
thus be negated, and he spoke vehemently against the
suggestion. It was, he thought, just another proof of the
growing power of the central government, utterly opposed to the states' rights theory and his own "concurrent
majority." He made fun of the suggestion of simply mark-
ing certain items "Expunged." He remarked, "They tell
us that the resolution on your records is not to be expunged, but is only to be endorsed 'Expunged.' Really,
sir, I do not know how to argue against such contemptible
sophistry."

The disposition of public lands in newly formed states
had been under discussion for many years. Calhoun had
a final run-in with the old general in the White House
over this issue. There was quite obviously a great deal of
speculation in government lands, and Calhoun said publicly that much of it was in high places in the government. Jackson accused him of personal slander and called

for a public apology. To Calhoun, whose guiding motive was honesty, this was incredible. He had never mentioned Jackson by name in his statement. Jackson had said in part, "I ask you, sir, . . . to retract this charge, or I shall give publicity to this letter by which you will stand stigmatized as one who . . . is ready to stab the reputation of others without the magnanimity to do them justice. . . ." Calhoun was astounded that Jackson could "place himself in a position so unworthy of his exalted station," and he repeated what he had said. "It has been frequently stated and not contradicted that many in high places are among the speculators . . . even an individual connected with the President himself. . . ."

Congress adjourned to meet again under the new President, Martin Van Buren, and Calhoun was freed for the moment from political battling. He looked forward to a brief respite at Fort Hill—the early-morning walks around the plantation, the cheery greetings of his faithful slaves and their reports on the condition of the crops and the cattle. He had developed into somewhat of an expert, and his inspections were always very thorough. Dinner was at three, and during the meal he would listen with interest to Floride describing the improvements she had made around the house and the garden. She had—and he smiled to himself as he thought of it—a passion for making additions to the house and rearranging the garden. He had confided to a friend once that he could always get the work done more cheaply, but it made Floride happy to do it, and that was all that really mattered.

His favorite son and daughter, Andrew and Anna Marie, were away. Andrew had married the daughter of his journalist friend Duff Green, and Anna Marie was married in 1838 to Thomas G. Clemson. Since 1844 she had been living in Brussels, where her husband had been appointed *chargé d'affaires* by President Tyler. The baby of the family, William Lowndes, his sister Cornelia and his three brothers, James, John and Patrick, would be there to welcome him. Although many of his political associates thought of him as a stern, dignified and humorless man, Calhoun knew the children felt differently, and he loved them for it. He fell asleep, his first night at Fort Hill, with no thought of slavery, petitions, land speculation or even Andrew Jackson.

There was a deep shadow over his homecoming. His mother-in-law, who had been like a second mother, died in 1836. She had befriended him thirty-two years before, and during all that time she had been a rich source of inspiration and encouragement. He was glad to be home with Floride in her sorrow, but momentous problems soon demanded his presence in Washington.

There were two boundaries yet unsettled in the new nation, that in the South and that in the far Northwest. In 1821, Mexico won her independence from Spain. The northern portion, known as Texas, was a fertile area of rich grassy plains and soon became the goal of wandering adventurers. Stephen Austin obtained an agreement from Mexico to start a colony, and soon there were 30,000 Americans living there, outnumbering the native Mexi-

cans four to one. All went well until the very different
temperaments of the two races began to clash, and fighting broke out in 1835.

Late in the fall of the next year, a small force of Americans was overwhelmed by the Mexicans at the Alamo, a
mission in San Antonio. This stimulated the Texans in
Washington to declare the independence of the "Republic of Texas," Sam Houston, a stalwart frontiersman and
former governor of Tennessee, was made commander-in-
chief of the Texas armed forces. After a series of defeats
at the hands of Santa Anna, he won a decisive victory at
the battle of San Jacinto, and the Lone Star Republic became a reality.

Here was an area as large as the whole of France neigh-
boring on the Southern states and containing soil ideally
suited to the growing of cotton. Southerners, including
Calhoun, looked on their new neighbor with jealous eyes.
The balance of power between the Northern antislavery
states and the Southern had been equally divided since
the admission of Arkansas. There was a large area north
of the Missouri Compromise line, including the disputed
Oregon land, that would unquestionably be divided into
states before very long; the South, with its "peculiar institution," would find itself a minority in Congress. Calhoun favored annexation of the new Republic and eventual admission into the Union.

Years before, he had stated his conviction that future
war with England was inevitable, and he still had a
lingering fear of that conflict. Texas, as a small Republic,

was wide open for conquest, which would bring British influence back to the Union in a formidable way. Also, the joint occupation of the Oregon territory with England since 1816 was a campaign issue in 1844, and hotheads were demanding that the boundary line should run through the latitude of 54° 40′ or else war would be declared.

To Calhoun, these two questions before the country were of vital importance. He wanted the annexation of Texas and a compromise with England on the Oregon boundary line. He envisaged an enlarged and strengthened Union, and he was willing to put all personal ambition aside to achieve this end. He had adherents to his cause in and out of Congress. Even his old enemy Andrew Jackson was strongly in favor of annexation, as were many others.

The endless debates on Texas in Congress went on through 1842, and there seemed to be no end in sight. Tyler's term was coming to its end, and already eager candidates were organizing their campaigns. Encouraged by such friends as Duff Green, Barnwell Rhett and George Pickens, Calhoun revived his interest in the Presidency. It had lain dormant for a year or two, while other issues were demanding his undivided attention. In November, 1842, he offered his resignation from the Senate, effective at the end of the Twenty-Seventh Session. As soon as this was known, South Carolina nominated him for President to succeed Tyler. With assurances of support from Alabama, North Carolina, New Hampshire,

Massachusetts and Michigan, and with British newspapers speaking of him as "one of the most remarkable
men in the United States," his hopes ran high that his
boyhood ambition might finally be realized.

But in the winter of 1845, Calhoun stubbornly refused
to play politics. He stated his polices freely to friend and
foe—free trade, low tariff, divorce of the central government from banking and a strict adherence to the Constitution. Thus, he alienated manufacturers, high-tariff men,
bankers and loose constructionists. Furthermore, the
abolitionist strength was increasing, and more and more
New York Democrats were supporting antislavery groups.
Calhoun also was openly opposed to nomination by a
National Convention, which he claimed would be run by
politicians. He saw and read correctly the road signs to
the White House. Duff Green, whose daughter had married Calhoun's son Andrew, was less meticulous when he
said, "What matter the party so long as your own advancement is assured." Always faithful to his principles,
Calhoun refused categorically to follow this advice, and
on December 21, 1843, he withdrew his name. His
friends regretted it but, knowing him, they understood.
One newspaper commented, "This act of Mr. Calhoun's
has done more to elevate him in the estimate of the good
and the hardworking than any act of his life."

The Texas discussions were still keeping Congress in
a turmoil, and Calhoun had followed them with intense
interest all through his abortive campaign. Abel P. Upshur, the Secretary of State, had completed an agreement

with the Texans which the latter hesitated to follow up
for fear of angering Mexico. They asked if the United
States would guarantee military and naval protection as
a part of the agreement. England and France were watch-
ing with eager eyes, and the situation was sensitive. Delay
was dangerous, but Upshur was hesitant about com-
mitting the administration to anything so radical. Just at
this point, Calhoun's whole system gave way. It was not
just weariness, although he was desperately tired. He had
been subject to bronchial weakness most of his life and
was constantly in fear of pneumonia. Back at Fort Hill,
he rested under the loving care of Floride and his 22-
year-old daughter, Cornelia. There were moments of
crisis, but his condition improved to a point where he
could carry on a correspondence with Congress and
others from his bed, and in a few months he was considering returning to Washington to add his voice to the
Texas discussion. Then a most unexpected and tragic
event occurred. President Tyler, Cabinet members and
friends, organized by Commodore Stockton of the Navy
were on an official pleasure cruise aboard the newly com-
missioned battleship *Princeton* when a gun exploded. The
President escaped injury, but Secretary of State Upshur
was killed, as was Virgil Maxey, the journalist, and David
Gardiner, a friend of Calhoun at Yale. It took many days
for the news of the accident to reach Fort Hill, and it did
little to boost Calhoun's failing spirits. He wrote letters
of condolence to the bereaved families in a rather shaky

hand and turned to other mail that had arrived by the same post.

He opened one bearing the Congressional seal and read it through in amazement. It informed him that, at the special request of President John Tyler, the Senate had confirmed the appointment of John C. Calhoun as Secretary of State following the tragic death of the incumbent, Abel P. Upshur.

He showed the letter to Floride, and they discussed it. Her interest in politics was slight, and the complications that were developing in national affairs merely confused her. She was flattered that her husband chose to discuss his problems with her, as he always did, and she contributed what suggestions she could. She had married a popular government figure of whom she was very fond and proud, and this letter was just another proof of the esteem in which he was held by the country's leaders. To Calhoun himself, it was not only complimentary, but a God-given chance to forward two of his pet projects, the annexation of Texas and the settlement of the Oregon boundary. Although he was sixty years old and afflicted with a chronic bronchial condition, his spirits were still at their peak, and it did not take him long to make up his mind. He left for Washington almost at once. The news of his appointment had spread, and he was royally entertained along the way at dinners and meetings, arriving in the Capitol on March 29 ready to take up his new duties. He had been Secretary of War and Vice President, but it

did not take much astuteness to show him that his present
post was more influential in forming basic governmental
policies than either of his previous positions.

The fatal explosion on the *Princeton* not only elevated
Calhoun to the office of Secretary of State but, in a round-
about way, elevated a charming young woman of thirty-
seven to the position of First Lady. Julia Gardiner, the
daughter of David Gardiner, an old friend of Tyler's and
one of the guests aboard the ill-fated *Princeton,* had for
some time been attracted by the twinkling blue-eyed,
light-haired, slender John Tyler. Her feelings were definitely reciprocated by the President. When she was told
on the battleship of her father's death, she promptly
swooned into the President's arms. Three months later,
on June 26, 1844, Miss Gardiner and John Tyler were
married. Later, at a formal banquet in honor of the
newlyweds, Calhoun found himself seated beside the
lovely Julia Tyler. He talked about her father with a
twinkle in his eye, telling anecdotes of undergraduate
life in New Haven. It was a most pleasant if somewhat
unusual interlude in his busy life, and he thoroughly
enjoyed it.

At his desk, he was faced with a most serious challenge.
Lying in front of him was an unanswered letter to Upshur from Richard Pakenham, the newly arrived British
minister, transmitting a dispatch from the British Foreign
Secretary, Lord Aberdeen. The dispatch was dated December, 1843, and it aroused deep resentment in the
honest mind of Calhoun. It was obviously intended to
soothe those in America who were suspicious of the Brit-

ish desire to interfere in the ultimate fate of the Republic of Texas. It was phrased in smooth diplomatic words, but to Calhoun's analytical mind, it clearly implied that Aberdeen's government would be quite willing to make every effort to secure Texas independence from Mexico and in return would guarantee the abolition of slavery. This idea was followed up by the inconsistent statement that while it was well known that the British wished to see slavery abolished throughout the world, they had no desire to interfere with the practice in any of the slave-holding states of the Union, unless the United States should attempt to annex Texas.

With his long-standing fear of more trouble with England, this was almost more than Calhoun could stand. He replied in language which, if not diplomatic in the accepted sense, was at least honest. He reminded Aberdeen that, in spite of his protestations of noninterference in Texas, the facts showed that the British had been interfering for a long time. He went on to say that the United States intended to annex Texas to assure their own security, and if there should arise any trouble between the United States and Britain, the latter would be guilty of starting it.

Upshur's treaty having been rejected by the Senate, Tyler and his Secretary of State resorted to the method of joint resolution, which bypassed the two-thirds rule. This was a shrewd move. The treaty was authorized, and just before his term expired, President Tyler signed it. Texas became an integral part of the American Union.

Calhoun had labored over the annexation of Texas and

still had the question of the Oregon boundary facing him, but personal problems still harassed him. After the "conic sections" incident at Yale, Andrew, his favorite son, had married and become a business partner of Anna Marie's husband, taking care of the latter's Alabama cotton plantation. This arrangement was not a complete success. Between Andrew's pleas to his father for help in supervising the plantation and Thomas Clemson's complaints from Belgium of Andrew's inefficiency, Calhoun faced a situation that would have completely discouraged most men. In spite of his demanding political duties, he found the time to help oversee Andrew's plantation and write soothing letters to Thomas Clemson. It was his nature to want to help the helpless, and there was no problem too large or too small for him to take over if it concerned his family or friends.

All news from Belgium, however, was not bad. Letters from Anna Marie were frequent, and he eagerly watched his mail for her rather scrawly handwriting. She was interested in all his problems, and her sense of humor often took the sharp edge off many of them. She had once confided to a friend, "Of course I do not understand as he does, for I am comparatively a stranger to the world, yet he likes my unsophisticated opinion, and I frankly tell him my views on any subject about which he inquires of me." He longed to see her, and it was a cruel fate that kept them so far apart.

⮌ IX ⮌

As March 4, 1845, approached and James K. Polk was about to become the eleventh President of the United States, Calhoun took stock of his future. It had been made quite clear to him that he was not wanted as Secretary of State in the new administration. He was sixty-three years old, and his health was definitely not the best. He had been able to secure the annexation of Texas with no condition as to slavery, but he had serious doubts as to Polk's handling of future relations with Mexico. The Oregon boundary was not yet settled, and Polk's insistence upon 54° 40′ threatened the war with England which Calhoun had for so long feared. There was the tariff question, since 1828 a difficult and unsolved problem. Relations with the West, river and rail improvements to create easy transportation between it and the South and, of course, the eternal question of slavery haunted him. One thing he was sure of. Following the inauguration, he would go

home and rest. After that? He would have to wait and
see.

March 4, 1845, was cold and rainy. Polk and Tyler
drove through umbrella-covered crowds. Calhoun and
other members of the Cabinet followed to the east portico
of the White House, where Polk delivered his inaugural
address. At the request of James Buchanan, the new Secretary of State, Calhoun remained with him for a week.
Before he left Washington, he called on the President to
bid him good-bye. Politics was not discussed at any
length, but Calhoun managed to drop the hint that he did
not approve of Polk's attitude towards Oregon. He was
visited at his hotel by all members of the new Cabinet
and was much touched by their warm farewells and good
wishes.

He had anticipated a quiet trip home, but at Richmond
he was tendered a dinner by James Ritchie, the editor of
the Richmond *Union*, and was flattered by the enthusiastic toasts, many of them making subtle reference to the
Presidential election of 1848. At Charleston, he was again
a guest of the city, but politely refused an invitation to a
public dinner. He wanted to get back to Floride and his
beloved Fort Hill. He would not take any actions or make
any public statements until he learned exactly how Polk
was going to act on many controversial issues, particularly that of the Oregon boundary.

He looked forward to several months of peace. He
would see the bare, red hills turn to heaps of white cotton
blossoms to be harvested and ginned in the fall. It would

bring back memories of when he himself plowed the furrows while his Negro hand followed, dropping in the precious seeds. It was the season for the white snow petals of dogwood, the yellow blaze of forsythia and the pungent odor of jasmine. From his porch he could see the sparkling waters of the Seneca River and the spire of the church in nearby Pendleton which he and Floride attended on Sundays. On long early-morning walks over the plantation, he would visit the cotton and corn fields, the slave quarters—perhaps to see a newborn baby or a sick hand—and the cattle pen, where he might inspect a recently acquired Devon bull. Reading, writing and long talks with Floride and the many friends who dropped in made up the rest of his day; after another walk in the evening, he retired early. He was working on a book on the government of the United States in which he hoped to sum up his various theories. It was the life he loved, and he would gladly have continued it indefinitely.

Unfortunately, there were momentous questions facing the country, and many friends and even enemies missed Calhoun's masterly logic and quiet common sense. The post almost daily brought letters urging him to accept a seat in the Senate. Senator Huger even offered to give up his seat if he could be assured that Calhoun would accept it, and Daniel Webster, his old friend and political enemy, was anxious to see him back. About this same time, he was chosen to preside at a convention in Memphis, Tennessee, called in an attempt to cement the South's relations with the growing West by the development of roads, canals and railroads. The convention was not a complete success, but it served as additional proof of his popularity all through the country. He was wined and dined all along the route to Tennessee, and was loudly cheered when he left the convention hall. All this added to the temptation to return to public life, particularly since the Democrats were losing control, which could lead to the frustration of his hopes of saving the South. However, he was wrestling with personal financial troubles. With the price of cotton on the decline and the cost of running the plantation remaining high in spite of his efficient management, his debts were mounting. Many of his friends offered loans. Even Daniel Webster, possibly not wishing to lose so skillful an opponent, joined the ranks of those offering help. In September, as the heavy carts were carrying the cotton to the gin mill, he agreed to be a candidate in spite of his personal troubles, writing his decision to his friend and relative, Francis Pickens. ". . . I feel that there is a heavy responsibility on me, in determining the course I should take. . . . I do not see, under all the circumstances, how I could decline the duty if it shall be the desire of the Legislature and the State. . . ." It was definitely the desire of the Legislature, and Calhoun was at once elected to fill the seat vacated by Senator Huger.

When he arrived in Washington, he faced a crisis which threatened not only the country but his personal hopes for Texas and Oregon. The Capitol was suffering from expansionist fever. The Oregon question was on everyone's mind, and the cry everywhere was "fifty-four forty or fight," encouraged by Polk's statement that if the nation couldn't acquire the whole of Oregon by treaty, it would take it by force. There were, however, saner minds. On hearing of Calhoun's decision to accept election, Mr. Pendleton rose in the House of Representatives to say, "I hope sincerely that he will be found on this occasion, where his large experience and matured wisdom make it almost certain that he must be found, on the side of peace, the peace of his own country and the world; that he will with all the strength of his great intellect resist the rash and ill-advised counsels that would plunge his country into war."

Mr. Pendleton need not have worried. To Calhoun, the seizure of Oregon by force would have been deliberate national suicide. Some years before, he had spoken against a similar bill. He had pointed out that England had troops in China and India which could be in Oregon in less than half the time it would take the United States to move an army either across the continent or around the Horn. The results, he said, could easily be predicted. The United States would lose the whole territory and the battle losses would be tragically great.

There were those, especially in the South, who looked upon the extreme Northwest as a useless, dried-up land of no real value, but Calhoun felt differently. He had taken the trouble to talk at length with many of the bronzed and tough-skinned pioneers who had made the long trek over the Rockies. They returned at intervals with tales of the potential of the Columbia River area. Calhoun was among those few who sincerely believed them, and he determined to take up the gauntlet. This meant, of course, opposing not only many of his friends in the South but the President himself. Ever since Tyler, with his Secretary of State Calhoun, had consummated the annexation of Texas, Polk had held a bitter grudge against the South Carolina Senator. Calhoun once told a friend that Polk could not in any way injure him and, convinced that he was right, he resolved to follow what might be a dangerous course.

Early in March, 1846, he asked for and was granted an opportunity to speak on the Oregon Bill, a joint resolution of the Committee on Foreign Relations proposing to give notice to Great Britain of the intention of this government to annul the treaty of joint occupation of the Oregon territory. Word soon spread that Calhoun was to oppose the President's bill advocating seizure of the Oregon Territory, and crowds began gathering near the Capitol early in the morning of March 16. His appearance was always a magnet for the public. Whether the individuals agreed with him or not, he was bound to be dramatic. The galleries were filling long before twelve o'clock, when the session would officially open.

Calhoun sat and watched. His thoughts went back thirteen years to the day he spoke against the "Force Bill." Then his beloved South had been threatened and the specter of a consolidated government rose to do away with states' rights. England had just abolished slavery, and this gave the abolitionists fresh ammunition in their battle to deprive the South of its "peculiar institution." Now the whole country was threatened by the possibility of war against the most powerful nation on earth. Some days before, Calhoun had said sadly, "I anticipate a severe seven months' campaign. I have never known our country in such a state. I will do all in honor I can do, but, after all, what can one man do?" What, indeed, could his voice do in opposition? Would his words and arguments bear any fruit, or would they be heard and ignored? The time came to find the answer. He rose, and the whispers and shuffling of feet suddenly ceased. The silence seemed to increase the tension in the small, crowded room. Calhoun was convinced that he was right. "I shall abstain," he began, "from everything of a personal character, and from everything calculated to wound the feelings of any gentleman, but at the same time, I shall express myself fully, freely and candidly on all the subjects involved."

He pointed out that those in favor of the notice were persuaded of two things—First, that the United States title to Oregon was valid and, second, that a compromise was impossible. Then he continued: "We are opposed to that notice because we do not agree with them in that opinion. We believe on the contrary that a compromise can be effected. . . . We do not think the American title to the whole of Oregon to be so perfectly clear as to be indisputable. We hold that the title of neither nation to

the whole country is perfect and, therefore, we do not
and cannot believe that two powerful and enlightened
nations . . . will go to war on such a question so long as
war can honorably be avoided."

He pointed out the dangers to the currency which
result from war, referring to what happened after the
Revolution and the War of 1812. He prophesied that,
should Great Britain be successful in this war, she would
undoubtedly pursue that success to the destruction of
the American Union.

> But I have higher reasons. I am opposed to war
> as a friend of human improvement. . . . Never in
> the history of the world has there occurred a period
> so remarkable as the peace that followed the battle
> of Waterloo for the great advances made in the con-
> dition of human society. The chemical and mechani-
> cal powers have been investigated and applied. . . .
> The invention of man has . . . subjugated two great
> agencies of the natural world. . . . I refer to steam
> and electricity. Steam has been controlled. . . . It
> has shortened the passage across the Atlantic more
> than one-half, while the rapidity of traveling on
> land has been three times greater than by the com-
> mon motive power. Within the same period man has
> claimed the very lightening of heaven and made it
> administer to the transmission of human thought.
> Magic wires are stretching in all directions over the
> globe. . . . Mighty means are now put into the hands

of England and the United States to cement and secure a perpetual peace by breaking down the barriers of commerce and uniting them in . . . an intercourse mutually beneficial. . . . And far more than that. An intercourse like that points to that inspiring day which philosophers have hoped for, which poets have seen in the bright visions of fancy and which prophecy has seen in holy vision—when man shall learn war no more. . . . Finally I am against war because peace—peace is preeminently our policy.

He had spoken out. His speech was long, over three triple-columned pages in the *Congressional Globe*, but he felt that he had not said a useless word and apparently his audience agreed with him. They had listened in silence, and as Calhoun sat down there was a burst of applause such as had not been heard in the Senate for a long time. Senators from both sides of the aisle hurried to his seat to shake him by the hand, and their congratulations were not just routine. There was a deep sincerity in every voice that spoke. He had shown himself to be a true American. There was no taint of prejudice or sectionalism in his words, but a powerful plea for the peaceful preservation of the Union. One political enemy told a friend, "Calhoun has covered himself with a mantle of glory."

Polk felt that Calhoun was playing politics and aiming for the Presidency. He knew he was defeated, and must make an attempt to save face. Congress ignored the

President's defiant notice to England, and instead authorized him to tender another offer of compromise. This Polk did, even offering the 49th parallel as the northern boundary. The President had capitulated, and now it was up to England. On her answer depended Calhoun's triumph. Would his words bear fruit, or would they turn out to be merely words?

April and May were months of agony to Calhoun. No word was received from England until their acceptance of the compromise in June. In the meantime, although he had been instrumental in bringing about the annexation of Texas, difficulties were piling up in relations with Mexico. In 1845, John Slidell, a New York–born lawyer twice defeated for a seat in the Senate but instrumental in securing the election of Polk, was sent to Mexico. His instructions were to further Polk's desire to finally adjust the Texas boundary and, if possible, purchase New Mexico and California. Mexico refused to receive him on the basis that his credentials were faulty. He was accredited as a full representative instead of merely for a single purpose. He returned to Washington.

After this rebuff and on the pretext of protecting Texas, Polk ordered troops under General Zachary Taylor to move to the Rio Grande from the Nueces. To Mexico this was an invasion of her territory, since she contended that the Nueces River formed the boundary of her lost state of Texas. This point of view had some merit, but it didn't appeal to Polk, and there was ominous talk of war. Calhoun dreaded a war with Mexico which would antagonize the British and possibly lead to a breakdown of the Oregon talks.

The fiery General Taylor had occupied the town of Punta Isabel on the Rio Grande near the coast and was waiting for trouble. The citizens of Matamoros just across the river listened to the Americans singing "Yankee Doodle" and "Hail Columbia," and they replied with guitar playing and Spanish songs. On April 25, 1846, a party of sixty American dragoons was ambushed by a Mexican force under General Arista, and all were killed or taken prisoner. General Taylor instantly called for a declaration of war on the basis of an enemy attack on the territory of the United States and sent for additional troops. The Mexican contention was, of course, that United States' authority ended with the Nueces River and that Mexico was simply repelling an attack—having already ordered the American troops back to the Nueces.

It was quite obvious which point of view would be accepted by President Polk, who declared unequivocally that "the cup of forbearance has been exhausted . . . . Mexico has passed the boundary of the United States . . . and shed American blood upon American soil. . . ." A war bill was offered in Congress. Calhoun was absent that day, and heard the news from Senator Clayton, who had forced him to vote on the famous Compromise Tariff Bill back in 1833. To Calhoun the proposal seemed incredible, and Clayton, knowing Calhoun's feelings on the subject, begged him to do something. On May 11, Calhoun heard the bill given its second reading, after which

it would be put to a vote. It called for two things—a declaration that war existed by act of Mexico and a request
for supplies to carry it on. The twofold nature of it confused Calhoun. He knew that by opposing the bill he
would be antagonizing not only the Administration but
many of his friends in both the North and the South.
Curiously enough, he would also be playing into the
hands of many abolitionists, who feared an extension of
slavery. He was confident of some support, though, from
his arch-foe Thomas H. Benton of Missouri, who had
already informed Polk personnally that he could not vote
for an aggressive war against Mexico.

On May 12, 1846, after listening to some routine business, Calhoun asked for the floor.

As he rose, it was obvious to all that he was older than
his years would indicate. His hands were almost bony
thin and his face was definitely care-worn, but those who
caught his eyes as he glanced around the Senate chamber
saw in them the same old courageous gleam of conviction. His gestures were as effective and restrained as
ever, and he wasted no words.

I have no disposition to create unnecessary delay
in the passage of this bill. . . . Why would not
gentlemen who desire unanimity agree to strike out
the preamble . . . and suffer the question of supplies to be separated from a declaration of war? I
am prepared to vote the supplies on the spot, and
without an hour's delay, but it is just as impossible

for me to vote for the preamble as it would be to plunge a dagger into my heart. . . . How does anyone know that the government of Mexico will not disavow what has been done? . . . It would be impossible for me to utter such a vote consistently with that sacred regard for truth in which I have been educated. . . . I have no certain evidence to go on.

He felt that to make war on Mexico by declaring war to exist before it had been Constitutionally declared, as the President was proposing, was equivalent to making war on the Constitution itself. His speech was short but decisive. He ended with a logical proposition—"To say that by a certain military movement of General Taylor and General Arista every citizen of the United States is made the enemy of every man in Mexico is monstrous. It gives that power to make war to every officer, nay to every subaltern commanding a corporal's guard. Do gentlemen call upon me to do that?"

He was followed at once by Senator Benton, who expressed much the same sentiment and asked that the bill be referred to the Military Affairs Committee for possible division of its two clauses. A vote was taken. The suggestion of Calhoun and Benton was defeated by a vote of 26–20, and the bill was passed in its original form. The next day, the President signed an official declaration of war against the Republic of Mexico. There was nothing for Calhoun to do but accept the inevitable, and hope that the news would not affect the British attitude towards the proposed compromise and that the war with Mexico would be short.

The war with Mexico not only was not short, but lasted for twenty-one months and created the most explosive issues. President Polk was a Virginia slaveholder, and quite naturally it was rumored that his desire to acquire Texas had been a wish to extend the boundaries of the slaveholding states. When, on August 8, 1846, three months after the outbreak of the war, he asked Congress for the sum of $2,000,000 to tempt Mexico into ending the war and ceding California to the United States, the rumor was strenthened. While there may have been a modicum of truth to the rumor, Polk's prime motive was protection of the borders of the Union against such potential intruders as England, France and Spain, which might conceivably ignore President Monroe's Doctrine.

The bill was considered in Congress, and there was much opposition to handing the President such a "blank check." Then an explosion occurred. David Wilmot, a relatively unknown representative from Pennsylvania, offered an amendment. The $2,000,000 should be authorized provided that, "as an express and fundamental condition to the acquisition of any territory from the Republic of Mexico by the United States by any treaty that may be negotiated between them and to the use by the Executive of the money herein appropriated, neither slavery nor involuntary servitude shall ever exist in any part of said territory except for crime whereof the party shall first be duly convicted." There was a small filibuster, and the bill and its amendment lost when, owing to a difference in clocks, the Senate adjourned ten minutes before the House.

But the writing on the wall was clear to Calhoun and his Southern friends. From now on the question of slavery could no longer be treated as a secondary issue. The sections were openly girding for battle. Control of Congress, with the admission of Iowa and the pending application of Wisconsin, was uncontestably with the North, and far-seeing Southerners saw with Calhoun an inevitable amendment to the Constitution abolishing slavery. The only barrier to this was to permit the South an equal voice in the settlement of any new territory below the Missouri compromise line, and this the Wilmot Proviso would forever prohibit. The measure was temporarily dead, but its spirit was still a blinding glare in the eyes of all Southerners. Their "peculiar institution" was being threatened on both moral and political grounds. This was no insignificant matter. The present generation had received the institution from its ancestors, and it was not one of their own making. Their economy, their very lives, depended on it. Take it away suddenly, and they would be reduced to an impoverished minority faced with the threat of bloody revolution.

In February, 1847, Calhoun expressed his personal feelings by presenting a series of resolutions. He did this, he said, to face the issue rather than let things take their course. In presenting his resolutions he stressed the fact that the states were united in a Federal Union under a

constitution which in unmistakable terms calls for justice
and equality. For some years, the votes of the Southern
and Northern states had been equally divided in Congress, but since 1820, when the Missouri Compromise
was effected, and somewhat later as new states above
the Compromise line were admitted, this equality had
been disturbed. The only end in sight, Calhoun said,
would be the complete dominance of the North over the
South. Where, then, he asked, is your equality—where
your justice? "If this should happen," he told the Congress, ". . . it is not for me to say what the South will do.
But I may speak as an individual member of the Union."

"In the South," he said, "is my family. . . . There I
drew my first breath; there are all my hopes. I am a
planter—a cotton planter. I am a Southern man and a
slaveholder—a kind and merciful one I hope—and none
the worse for being a slaveholder. I say, for one, I would
rather meet any extremity than give up one inch of our
equality—one inch of what belongs to us as members of
this great Republic. . . . I think I can see the future. If
we do not stand up as we ought, in my humble opinion
. . . the condition of Jamaica is happy and prosperous
compared with what must be that of the Southern states."

Calhoun was definitely a kind and merciful slaveholder. The system was part of a status quo which, if
suddenly abandoned, would bring about untold con-
fusion. In a discussion in 1816 on a question of a commercial treaty with England, he had referred to the
slave trade as "that odious traffic." He remembered with

pleasure his old fishing companion, Sawney, and at one time he released two of his slaves to permit them to work in the North. In a very short time, they begged him to let them return to the plantation. The slavery question, like the tariff discussions, was to be solved by what he had consistently called the rule of a concurrent majority rather than that of a completely dominating majority. He feared the potential of this majority as a threat to the South, and he was determined to center his attention on his own state of South Carolina. There was no doubt that the danger was growing and the mere fact that Wilmot's amendment was temporarily on the shelf meant nothing. The idea had been definitely planted in the minds of both abolitionists and Northern politicians, and the only remedy would be in the hands of a united South, anxious only to defend its rights as a group of constituent parts of a federal government.

X

After a month and a half of the Mexican War, England agreed to the Oregon compromise on June 18, 1846, and Calhoun was relieved of one of his many worries. It was clearly an honorable settlement. Actual occupation by American settlers was entirely below the 49th parallel, and British pride was apparently assuaged.

In the meantime, the war with Mexico went on. Calhoun followed it with disapproving eyes, resenting the expenditure of money and the needless bloodshed on both sides over a boundary issue that could have been settled by compromise. In the Senate, Truman Smith of Connecticut said with considerable heat a month after the war that it had been begun "unnecessarily and un-Constitutionally by the President." Over in the House there was a thirty-eight-year-old Representative from Illinois, elected in 1846. He was a Republican and strongly antislavery, but he agreed wholeheartedly with

154

Calhoun on the policy of the Mexican War. It was one of the few things they agreed on. The young man's name was Abraham Lincoln.

Many of Calhoun's friends who held opposite opinions chided him with a reminder of his War Hawk days back in 1811. His answer was clear and logical. For four years beginning in 1807, England had been subjecting American sailors to seizure by impressment in the British navy, desperate for fighting men. They had been warned repeatedly, but the insult to American citizens was continued. In this case, war was the only answer if the United States was to maintain its integrity in the eyes of the world. The Mexican situation, he felt, was far different. The expansionist sentiment had turned the heads of the majority of American citizens, even going so far as a plan to seize all of Mexico and add it to the Union. The difficulty of absorbing a nation already thickly populated with members of a Latin race never seemed to occur to them. Calhoun remembered what most expansionists seemed to have forgotten, that the incompatibility of the two races was what led to the declaring of independence by the Texas colony in 1836.

The war was a rather strange one. Mexico, apparently realizing too late her loss of Texas, was making a completely futile effort to recover it, or at least the disputed territory between the Nueces and the Rio Grande. The United States, instead of being satisfied with the state of Texas and the disputed area as Calhoun was continually urging, followed the boastful Polk and the expansionists.

The outcome was never too much in doubt. Mexico was in a state of almost continual revolution, with constant changes of presidents, and could hardly be called a formidable foe.

The United States, on the other hand, motivated by expansionist ambition and backed up by a number of capable officers filled with the extreme pioneering spirit of the time and the hope of floating into the Presidency on a stream of victories, held the winning cards. She played them to the hilt, and was victorious in every battle. General Winfield Scott of Virginia captured the seaport of Vera Cruz in March, 1847, largely through the skill of another young Virginian, Robert E. Lee. Santa Fe, New Mexico, fell to an American force under Colonel Philip Kearney, who promptly claimed the area of Utah, Arizona and Nevada for the United States. California had already been declared United States territory by Commander John D. Sloat after he won a signal victory at Monterey. Antonio López de Santa Anna, the deposed president, who had been exiled to Cuba and allowed through the blockade at Vera Cruz on his promise to secure the best terms, reneged on his word and raised a conglomerate army of 6,000,000 or 7,000,000 Indians, half-breeds and whites to oppose the United States. In spite of his unquestioned military ability, he was unable to halt the march of General Scott and young Robert E. Lee, who followed the route of Hernando Cortes and his conquistadores across Mexico, past the towering peak of Popocatepetl and the sleeping woman mountain, Ixtaccihuatl, into the broad Mexican valley. After three or four brilliant victories, the Americans seized and held the presidential palace of Chapultepec. To all intents and purposes the war was over.

Calhoun followed the war with a troubled mind. The cry to hold the whole of Mexico in bondage was still being heard from many hotheads, but fortunately more sober voices, among them Calhoun's were more powerful. A treaty was signed on February 2, 1848, which left Mexico alone except for the cession of New Mexico and California. The United States agreed to pay all claims against Mexico by American citizens and so ended the problem of further southern expansion and the addition of some 1,000,000 square miles of territory to the United States.

Ever since his Senate speech of May 12, 1846, critical of the administration's proposal of aggressive war against Mexico, Calhoun was thoroughly conscious of the fact that his lifelong dream of reaching the Presidency had faded forever. He had consistently refused to play politics. The word "expediency" was not in his vocabulary. If his convictions did not lead him to the Presidency, that was God's will, and he would not dispute it. He clung, however, to his resolution to defend the rights of the agrarian South against the industrial North. As his physical strength ebbed, his inner convictions seemed to flow more strongly. There were still battles to be fought in Congress, where his Northern opposition was growing stronger. He knew that he must strive to unite the South and give strength to its demands for an equal say in all legislation.

In March of 1847, at the end of the Twenty-Ninth Session of Congress, with the war at its height, he addressed a huge gathering of the citizens of Charleston. He had a severe cold and his doctor had advised him not to use his voice, but he knew very well that his voice was his only remaining weapon with which to fight. He had a little difficulty at first, but he forced himself.

"My fellow citizens," he began, "in complying with the request of your committee to address you on the general state of our affairs in connection with the federal government, I shall restrict my remarks to our peculiar domestic institution not only because it is by far the most important to us but also because I have fully expressed my views in my place in the Senate on the only other important subject—the Mexican War. . . . After all that has occurred during the last twelve months, it would be almost idiotic to doubt that a large majority of both parties in the nonslaveholding states have come to a fixed determination to appropriate all the territories of the United States, now possessed or hereafter to be acquired, to themselves to the entire exclusion of the slaveholding states."

He pointed out the danger of the antislavery sentiment in the North, which could easily turn the scales in favor of the Wilmot Proviso. "The political leaders in the North," he continued, "care little about slavery, but they are willing to curry favor with the abolitionist voters in order to achieve political advancement, many with an eye on the Presidency. . . . Let us show at least as much spirit in defending our rights and honor as they have evinced in assailing them. Henceforward let all party distinctions cease . . . as long as this aggression on our rights and honor shall continue. . . . Let us regard every man as of our party who stands up in its defense." He assured them that the nonslaveholding states, fearful of losing the votes of so unified a group, would let the matter drop in order to achieve their political ends. "Our object is to preserve the Union if it can be done consistently with our rights, safety and perfect equality. On this we have a right to insist. Less we cannot take."

He had taken a stand he would maintain to the end of his life. He was fully prepared to hear his motives challenged, and indeed they were. It was widely proclaimed that he was urging the complete dissolution of the Union. It was true that he saw this possibility and had seen it from the start, but far from urging it he had consistently fought for means to prevent it. His theory of rule by a concurrent majority would, he maintained, hold the Union together, and at the same time strengthen the rights of the individual states. He felt sincerely that he was more pro-Union than the Northern politicians who were hoping to disrupt the economy of half the states. As if this were not a charge difficult enough to bear, Northern rumor had it that he was motivated by an inordinate desire to assume the Presidency. It was true, he told himself, that ever since his entrance into politics he had held that as a possible goal, but not at the sacrifice of honest convictions. On the contrary, he had often opposed the administration in power, and even disagreed wholeheartedly with both Southern and Northern friends —all potential voters.

Calhoun was astute enough to know that after the partial failure of the attempt made at Memphis to bring the West and South together, the only remaining answer was a complete consolidation of the South. His address to the citizens of Charleston was the opening gun of his new attack, and he found he had considerable support. The Southern states appeared to be united in opposition to the Wilmot Proviso—especially South Carolina, Virginia and Mississippi. Jefferson Davis of Mississippi and Barnwell Rhett of South Carolina, both younger men, sensed the need of a united South as deeply as Calhoun. Calhoun had already confided his thoughts to Anna Marie Clemson, his favorite daughter. Speaking of the Wilmot amendment, he wrote: "The present indication is that the South will be united in opposition to the Scheme. If they regard their safety they must defeat it even if the Union should be rent assunder. . . . I desire above all things to save the whole, but if that cannot be to save the portion where Providence has cast my lot."

In December of 1847, the Thirtieth Congress convened in Washington. Although Wilmot's amendment had been defeated, Congress had been divided and the basic question of slavery in the newly acquired territories was very much alive. When Calhoun arrived in Washington and took his seat, his heart was heavy. He knew perfectly well that again he would play the part of a "loner," and he wondered if his failing strength would permit him to battle his opponents successfully. The disposition of an enormous extent of land was in dispute, and it irrevocably concerned the basic question of the rights of the people of the slave states. In a letter to Anna Marie, he said: "I look forward to the next session of Congress as one pregnant of events of the most momentous character."

In the last Congress, he had hoped to bring his resolutions to a vote, but pressure of final business caused them to be tabled. Thomas H. Benton, who had sided with him on the Mexican War issue, referred to them as idle abstractions.

In spite of the seeming indifference of Congress towards his resolutions, Calhoun was encouraged by the feeling of unity in the South which had been growing since late in 1847. Meetings were held, and resolutions passed by many of the Southern state legislatures advocated much the same claims as those made by him. In one instance, it was even proposed that should the Wilmot Proviso be passed, all Southern members of Congress would walk out and "return to their constituents." In all these protests, however, the dissolution of the Union was looked upon as a desperate last resort. Such expressions as "We love the Union; we cherish for it a sacred fondness and affection" were common in most of the speeches and resolutions, but the alternative, the "degradation" of the Wilmot Proviso, was something that no Southerner would put up with.

The Oregon question held priority in the new session. The territory badly needed some form of government and federal aid as it was harassed by violent incursions of the Cayuse Indians and had no force sufficient to combat them. Marcus Whitman, a pioneer and missionary who had established a mission there, was cruelly massacred with his wife and children. Calhoun was fully in accord with the need for some form of government in Oregon, but he was quite aware of the broader issues. Senator Douglas, who had been Calhoun's host at the Memphis meeting, proposed that the form of government in the territory should be left up to the inhabitants, a plan dubbed "Squatter Sovereignty" by its opponents. Calhoun regarded this as more dangerous than the Wilmot Proviso, claiming that it brought up dangerous constitutional questions. It was also suggested that the Missouri Compromise bill should be extended to the Pacific.

Calhoun looked upon these proposals as attacks on the rights of the Southern states. He reasoned that they not only were aimed at curbing the system of slavery but also, almost more important to the South, in a subtle way attempted to exclude slaveholding citizens from an enormous newly acquired territory, thus enhancing the Congressional power of the Northern states. He envisioned, as he had for years, the possibility of a majority in Congress passing an amendment to the Constitution prohibiting slavery. "Be assured," he said at one time, "if there be stern determination on one side to exclude us, there will be determination still sterner on ours not to be excluded." He added, most prophetically, "The day the balance between the two sections is removed will not be far distant from revolution, anarchy, civil war, and widespread disaster."

The Oregon Bill included a rider prohibiting slavery—not unlike the Mexican war proposal, which had also contained two distinct parts in one package. Calhoun was perfectly familiar with the fact that Oregon territory was physically inappropriate for the agricultural work of slaves, but by passing the bill with the slavery clause, Congress would be excluding any slaveholder who might choose to emigrate to Oregon with his property. In reply to Senator Dix of New York, who had accused him of a desire to extend the area of slavery, he said, "We are not contending for any extension. . . . What we do contend for is that the Southern states, as members of our Union, are entitled to equal rights and equal dignity, in every respect with the Northern, and that there is nothing in the Constitution to deprive us of that equality in consequence of our being slaveholders."

Discussion of Oregon—and by inference, of course, all newly acquired territory—reached the boiling point in June, 1848. Squatter Sovereignty, the Missouri Compromise, slavery exclusion and Constitutional rights were all attacked and defended. Early in the session, Calhoun had made a brief statement of his attitude towards the territories. He said, "The territory of Oregon is the territory of the United States, and by the United States we mean the states in their federal capacity as members of the Union. I rest it upon the additional fact that the states in their federal capacity are equal and coequal, and being so, no discriminations can exist between those who hold slaves and those who do not." Then, on June 27, he spoke at length. He knew that he had said much of what he had to say before, but it had to be repeated. It was increasingly clear to him that he was fighting a losing battle—not only for the cause of the South but also for his own life—but he would not give up.

His speech was long and naturally repetitive, for there was really nothing new for him to say. His opening remarks, however, emphasized the simplicity and fairness of what he was asking.

"Have the Northern states," he asked, "the power which they claim, to exclude the Southern from emigrating freely with their property into territories belonging to the United States, and to monopolize them for their exclusive benefit?"

It is indeed a great question. I propose to discuss it calmly and dispassionately. I shall claim nothing that does not fairly and clearly belong to the Southern states either as members of the Federal Union, or in their separate and individual character; nor shall I yield any. . . . I am influenced by neither sectional nor party considerations. If I know myself, I would repel as promptly and decidedly any aggression of the South on the North, as I would any on the part of the latter on the former. And let me add, I hold the obligation to repel aggression to be not much less solemn than that of abstaining from aggression, and that the party that submits to it when it can be resisted to be not much less guilty and responsible for consequences than that which makes it. Nor do I stand on party grounds. What I shall say in reference to the subject, I shall say entirely without reference to the Presidential election. I hold it to be infinitely higher than that and all other questions of the day. I shall direct my efforts to ascertain what is constitutional, right and just under a thorough conviction that the best and only way of putting an end to this, the most dangerous of all questions to our Union and institutions, is to adhere rigidly to the Constitution and the dictates of justice. . . .

Justice under the Constitution, rule by concurrent majority and the preservation of the Union was what he was pleading for in and out of Congress, sacrificing his health to achieve his goal. Two months after this last appeal, the Oregon question was settled and a territorial government was formed which excluded slavery. The system, Calhoun knew, as well as anyone, could not physically exist in Oregon or any Northwest territory, but the Northern politicians had won a technical but vital point, and there would now be no limit to which they might not go. Calhoun sadly noted this, and said to a friend, "The separation of the North and South is completed."

~ XI ~

Calhoun now saw clearly that there were no longer two or even three political parties, but two separate and distinct nations. The Union, for the formation of which his fellow countrymen had given their lives and for the preservation of which he had devoted the greater part of his life, was split asunder. As in the case of a critically injured accident victim, everything possible had to be done to preserve its life.

In December and into January, meetings were held of all Southern congressmen, regardless of nominal party affiliations. Calhoun was made chairman, and he drew up an address which was to be distributed widely to all their constituents. It was a comprehensive statement of the South's grievances against the North. There was a definite tone of desperation, starting with the economic unfairness of the Tariff of 1828, the unconstitutionality of the refusal of many states to return fugitive slaves and the proposal to abolish slavery in the District of Colum-

167

bia, and forseeing the enfranchising of the Negro as a
vote-getter for the Northern politicians. The members
were urged to forget all party lines, and unite in order
to prevent "a carnival of profligacy and bottomless degradation." It was even proposed that there should be two
presidents to defend the interests of both sections. The
meetings were well attended, but were not as completely
successful as Calhoun had hoped. Many Southern Senators, including Sam Houston of Texas and David Toombs
of Georgia, preferred their Whig alignment, thinking it
a better way to save the Union than through more risky
measures. Here Calhoun differed dramatically. What was
risk with the preservation of the Union at stake? Perhaps
it was because he saw the end of his life more clearly than
the younger men saw theirs and longed to see justice done
before his pleading voice would be silenced by death.
There were lengthy arguments and radical proposals, including a call by South Carolina and Mississippi for a
Southern Convention, but no definite conclusion was
reached other than to emphasize the growing danger.
The address was later printed in the Washington *Union*.

On January 17, Calhoun was in his seat in the Senate
listening to a discussion of an issue that momentarily replaced all others, the rush of gold seekers to the area of
Sutter's Mill in California. The sudden discovery of
gold was intriguing and he paid close attention, but his
mind was filled with worries. He was deeply disap-
pointed in the lack of unanimity in the recent meetings;
Zachary Taylor had just been elected the twelfth Presi-

dent of the United States over Lewis Cass, and there were strong indications that he was completely under the control of the Whig element. Perhaps, Calhoun thought, the South should have stood behind Cass, who was less opposed to the slaveholding states. His head ached a little, but that was not unusual. A senator was holding forth on the possibility of mob violence in California. As he finished, Calhoun rose to present a motion to use federal troops to protect the gold fields. He listened for someone to second his motion, but instead he heard a strange humming sound, his headache became almost unbearable and the room was suddenly blacked out.

Moments later, he opened his eyes. He was on a cot in the Vice President's room, and his friend Barnwell Rhett was leaning over him. What had happened was only too clear, and he whispered to Rhett, "I guess my career is reaching its end." Rhett encouraged him, telling him that the South needed him more than ever. The attack was soon over, and the next day he was in his seat taking some part in debate, but he fainted twice more and was forced to stay in his boardinghouse. He wrote encouragingly to Anna Marie and his family and looked forward to the end of the session and a return to Fort Hill. On the advice of friends, he was subjected to what was popularly called the "wet sheet treatment," which consisted of being wrapped in a damp sheet and covered with a pile of blankets for over an hour. He wrote to his daughter that "the process was soothing and pleasant," and by the end of May he was able to go home to Pendleton.

The summer was a happy one. He was with Floride, the wet season had brought the crops to fruition, the surrounding forests were becoming a rich green and the jasmine and dogwood had never been more beautiful. He took morning and evening walks as usual, although they were shorter than in the old days. He had great faith in his overseer and was able to devote a great deal of time to a project on which he had already worked for three years, a treatise on the Elementary Principles of the Science of Government.

There was, however, a serious blot on his vacation. In June, Senator Foote sent him a copy of a speech delivered at Jefferson City, Missouri, by Thomas Hart Benton. It was a most virulent attack on Calhoun and obviously demanded an answer. Benton, as a possible candidate of the Free Soil Party, was not exactly a hero in his home state, which leaned heavily to the cause of the South. On May 20, he undertook to win over his constituents by destroying the character of the Southern leader. He criticized his every move, claiming that Calhoun distorted historical facts for his own benefit, that his goal was the destruction of the Union, that the Wilmot Proviso should be called the Calhoun Proviso and that Calhoun's primary objective was the Presidency. He closed by saying, "Mr. Calhoun came into public life to be President of the United States. The weird sisters in the shape of the old man that taught him grammar whispered in his ear, 'Thou shalt be President.'"

This was so obviously a grudge speech, brimming over

with jealousy that dated from 1843, that Calhoun at first felt no obligation to answer it; but when on sober thought he realized that the attack made on him was in reality an indirect attack on the whole South, he decided to reply. On July 13, his answer appeared in the Pendleton *Messenger* and was quickly reprinted all over the country. His Phi Beta Kappa debating days and his many verbal duels with Webster and Randolph stood him in good stead. In a preliminary paragraph he said in part, "He seems to think I stand in his way. . . . On the contrary I have never for a moment thought of raising him to the level of a competitor." He then launched into a complete denial of all Benton's charges, sometimes ridiculing them and then disproving them by sober facts. His reply was well received in both North and South, but the whole affair failed to affect the cleavage between free and pro-slavery states.

Aside from this incident, Calhoun enjoyed his stay at home and found it too short. Duty always held priority over pleasure, and as the year 1849 drew to a close, he was back in Washington to continue the battle for Southern rights. In reply to a curt question about the South's intentions early in the session, he said, "I have long labored faithfully—faithfully—to repress the encroachments of the North. At the commencement, I saw where it would end and must end. I despair of ever seeing it arrested in Congress. It will go to its end. . . . Sir, what the South will do is not for me to say. They will meet it as it ought to be met."

Time after time the notation was made on the record,
"Mr. Calhoun resumed his seat this morning after his
severe indisposition." There was no doubt that he was
weaker. He was described by one senator as "altogether a
venerable man with a hard, stern, Scotch-Irish face, softened in its expression around the mouth by a sort of sad
smile which wins the hearts of all who converse with him.
His hair is snow white. He is tall, thin and angular. He
reminds you very much of Old Hickory." He was compelled to admit his weakness to himself, but he decided
on one last appeal. At his request, Henry Clay assigned
March 4, 1850, as the day on which the Senator from
South Carolina would speak. This was all that was needed
to fill the galleries. The ladies of Washington were definitely in the majority; the former Vice President and
Cabinet member was always a drawing card. All eyes
were turned towards the door as Calhoun came in on the
arm of his friend James Hamilton. He walked erect, head
held high, but as he reached his seat next to Jefferson
Davis, he sank into it with evident relief. Certain formali-
ties were quickly dispensed with, and Henry Clay turned
over the privilege of the floor to the Senator from South
Carolina.

Calhoun rose a little shakily, but once on his feet he
straightened up, and his voice was firm. He thanked the
Senate for its courtesy in permitting him the opportunity
of speaking at length. "Acting under the advice of
friends," he continued, "I have reduced to writing what I
intended to say, and without further remark, I will ask

the favor of my friend, the Senator behind me, to read it."
He sat down, wrapped a shawl around his shoulders and
glanced up with a smile of acknowledgement at his friend
James Murray Mason of Virginia, who had risen with a
paper in his hand.

"I have, Senators," Mr. Mason read in a firm voice
somewhat reminiscent of Calhoun at his best, "believed
from the first that the agitation of the subject of slavery
would, if not prevented by some timely and effective
measures, end in disunion. Entertaining this opinion, I
have on all proper occasions endeavored to call the attention of each of the two great parties that divide the country to adopt some means that will prevent such disaster.
The agitation has reached a period where it can no longer
be disguised or denied that the Union is in danger. You
have, then, had forced upon you the greatest and gravest
question that can ever come under your consideration.
How can the Union be preserved?" He reminded them
that he had endeavored time after time to persuade Congress to adopt measures to preserve it, but his voice was
not heeded. The Constitution calls for the return of fugitive slaves, but it has not been enforced.

Mr. Mason read on in the heavy silence, the written
word being occasionally accented by a gesture from Calhoun, whose eyes roved from face to face noting the varying reactions. It was not only the agitation on the slavery
question, he had written, but other issues, religious as
well as political, that threatened the Union. The cords of
unity had broken in the Methodist-Episcopal Church,

and the Baptist Church was showing signs of disunion. In politics the cry of 'Union, Union, the glorious Union' could no more save it than the cry of 'Health, Health, glorious Health' could save a dying man. There were growing signs of a loss of equilibrium between the sections. The census of 1820 showed an almost exact numerical division between the North and the South. Twenty years later, the North had a population preponderance over the South of almost 2,500,000; of the 222 members of the House of Representatives, the North had 135 and the South 87. The North was definitely taking over complete control of the government, changing it from a Federal Republic, as it originally came from the hands of its framers, into a great National Democracy as absolute as the autocracy of Russia. Revenue from duties was mostly absorbed by the North and Northern manufacturers, depriving the South of millions of dollars. The government was appointed as the common agent of all the states and charged with the interest and security of all, but it was disregarding the rights of a vast number of sovereign states. All the South asked was Justice. Let the North concede equal rights in newly acquired territory, let her enforce the fugitive slave law, let her cease the agitation of the slave question and let an amendment be added to the Constitution guaranteeing to the South the carrying out of these rights.

It was an earnest plea for fairness to a minority group phrased sincerely and logically, and it ended on a note of reluctant finality. "Having faithfully done my duty

both to the Union and to my section throughout this agitation, I shall have the consolation, let what will come,
that I am free from all responsibilty."

Back at Hill's Mess, his boarding place, he thought over
what he had done. Hill's Mess was in the building used
by Congress when the British had destroyed the Capitol
during the War of 1812. At that time, he had almost de-
spaired of saving the Union from a foreign enemy; now,
thirty-eight years later, he found himself again in despair
of saving it, but this time from an enemy within.

A compromise on the whole question which would
admit California as a free state, allow squatter sovereign-
ity to decide the issue in Utah and New Mexico, forbid
the slave trade in the District of Columbia and enforce
the fugitive slave law had been proposed by Henry Clay.
To Calhoun, this was not ideal; but at least it was a partial solution, and he would wait to hear how it would be
received in Congress. California had submitted her constitution, which declared her a free state, to President
Taylor, and day after day in Congress a decision was
being postponed. To the surprise of all, Webster spoke
eloquently in favor of the Compromise. By the middle
of March, it seemed inevitable that it would pass, which
it did six months later.

The sessions were becoming increasingly difficult for
Calhoun, and he attended only when he had the strength.
One day towards the end of March, Senator Foote, thinking Calhoun absent, launched into a long speech critical
of his motives and actions, saying that he himself would

never follow a leader and certainly not a disunionist. At this point, Calhoun, who had quietly taken his seat, interrupted Foote to say that he objected to remarks made during his absence and especially a charge so serious. He denied it and added, "I have never pretended to be the leader of any man."

As March drew to its close, he remained in his lodgings attended by a clerk, his son John and his loyal friend and doctor, Abraham Venable. He wrote encouraging letters to Floride lest she be alarmed, and he talked with friends. Discussing slavery with James Mason, he confided that his worst fears were not about his own suffering and possible death, but about his beloved Union. "The Union is doomed to dissolution; there is no mistaking the signs. . . . I fix its probable occurrence within twelve years or three presidential terms."

On Saturday, March 30, he found difficulty in speaking, and his breathing was extremely labored. On Sunday morning, he awoke around five o'clock. His son was by his bedside, and several of his closest friends were in the room. He smiled at them, but was unable to speak. He lay still, staring at the ceiling. His eyes grew tired, and he closed them. Then, instead of the ceiling, he seemed to see a series of pictures. They were confused and had little relation to each other. Floride as a little girl melded into the Floride he had last seen; the burning Capitol in Washington became a blazing bush of forsythia. Then he was standing alone on a platform condemning the British insults to the Union, and hearing

Senator Benton cruelly accusing him of urging the destruction of the same Union. The pictures faded, and he heard the pleading voice of the South change to a challenge. He seemed to hear the roar of cannon and the crashing of walls. Then there was silence and darkness.

EPILOGUE

On Monday, April 1, 1850, the Senate Chamber in Washington was strangely silent. There were no vote-getting arguments, no violent proclamations of the merits of favorite bills. The members stood in groups talking in hushed whispers or sitting silently in their seats. The news was not yet official, but the word had spread. The voice of South Carolina would never again be heard; the generous, pleading words in defense of the South, so full of sincere compassion and patriotism, would be only memories.

On a motion from the floor, the reading of the minutes was dispensed with, and Senator Butler of South Carolina addressed the Senate.

Mr. President: I rise to discharge a mournful duty and one which involves in it considerations well calculated to arrest the attention of this body. It is to announce the death of my late colleague, the Hon.

John Caldwell Calhoun. He died at his lodgings in this city yesterday morning at half past seven o'clock. He was conscious of his approaching end, and met death with fortitude and uncommon serenity. With his usual aversion to professions, he said nothing for mere effect on the world, and his last hours were an exemplification of his life and character, truth and simplicity."

Then Senator Butler traced Calhoun's life, stressing his services to his country as Representative, Cabinet member and Vice President, his ability as an orator, his dignity of purpose, the clearness, simplicity and utter sincerity of his words and his frank, kindly manner as a neighbor and friend.

Senator Butler was followed by other members, including Mr. Clay, Mr. Webster, Mr. Rusk and Mr. Clemens. Mr. Clay in late years had differed violently with Calhoun on matters of internal policy. In his speech he admitted this, but added: ". . . No man with whom I have ever been acquainted exceeded him in habits of temperance and regularity and in all the freedom, frankness and affability of social intercourse, and in all the tenderness and respect and affection which he manifested towards that lady who now mourns more than any other the sad event which has just occurred."

Mr. Webster, perhaps Calhoun's strongest opponent in debate, expressed the same sentiments, and the simplicity of his words vouched for the sincerity of their meaning.

Resolutions were passed to attend the Washington funeral at twelve the next day, and the Senate adjourned. The same proceedings took place in the House of Representatives, and similar resolutions were passed. The funeral was held, and the body placed temporarily in the Congressional Burying Ground. South Carolina was to be Calhoun's last resting place.

The speakers left no doubt of the universal admiration in which the late senator was held. The words "active," "ardent," "patriotic," "kindly," "devoted" and "honorable" were on everyone's lips.

April 1, 1850, was no ordinary day in the city of Charleston, South Carolina. Word had been received of the death of Senator Calhoun. The reaction was immediate. All business stopped. There was a grim silence in the streets, broken only by the slow tolling of the bell on St. Michael's Church. The ships in the harbor lowered their flags and raised them to half-mast. A son had lost a devoted father. His great devotion had perhaps never been fully realized, and now there remained only formal ceremonies as a means of showing appreciation and understanding.

These began with the arrival of the steamship *Nina* from Washington bearing the body of their hero. Never in the history of Charleston had there been such a demonstration of love and admiration as followed. Soldiers, school children, members of secret societies, foreign dignitaries, state governors and a host of citizens on horseback assembled to conduct the body to the City Hall.

Floride and her sons rode in carriages immediately behind the casket. To the measured roll of drums, the long
procession wound through the streets of Charleston. At
City Hall, the body remained in state for a day, watched
over by a guard of honor and visited by thousands. On
the 26th of April, funeral services were held in St. Philips'
Church, and the iron coffin was lowered into the vault
erected in the church cemetery. A stone slab, bearing the
simple word "Calhoun," was set in place. The door was
finally closed on the only man who could conceivably save
the country from sectional strife—whether by concurrent
majority rule, dual presidency or some compromise that
might be conceived in his fertile brain.

"I fix the date of dissolution of the Union at twelve
years or three presidential terms," he had said shortly
before his death.

The first presidential term was filled by a New York
moderate Whig, Millard Fillmore. He took a middle
course on the question of slavery, signed the Compromise of 1850 and sincerely tried to enforce the Fugitive
Slave law.

He was followed by Franklin Pierce, a rather mediocre
man from New Hampshire who leaned towards the South
but incurred the wrath of the North when he favored
squatter sovereignty in the disputed Kansas-Nebraska
area. Sectional difficulties became more explosive than
ever. Pierce was defeated in 1857 by James Buchanan of
Pennsylvania, who disapproved of slavery, but held to
the theory of squatter sovereignty. In the first year of his

office, a proslavery constitution was adopted for Kansas, and Buchanan tried to persuade Congress to admit Kansas under this measure, but it was defeated in 1858. The cord of union was wearing very thin, and there was no conciliating voice to strengthen it. Buchanan rashly promised South Carolina that there would be no coercion, but when Major Anderson moved his forces from Fort Moultrie to Fort Sumter, a far stronger position, the President was accused of breaking his promise. The move was a purely precautionary one, but South Carolina had another interpretation and on December 20, 1860, the delicate cord was at last broken. South Carolina seceded from the Union, demanding all federal forts within the state.

Buchanan left office the next year and fifty-two-year-old Abraham Lincoln entered the White House. The three Presidential terms prophesied by Calhoun were complete, and on April 12, 1861, cannon shots from South Carolina shattered the walls of Fort Sumter even as they had resounded eleven years before in the ears of the dying prophet—John Caldwell Calhoun.

BIBLIOGRAPHY

Alexander, H. M.	*The Famous Five*	New York: The Book-mailer, 1958.
Bancroft, Frederic	*South Carolina & Nullification*	Baltimore: Johns Hopkins Press, 1928.
Bates, Mary	*Private Life of John C. Calhoun*	Charleston, 1852.
Calhoun, J. C.	*Papers of*—ed. by R. L. Meriwether & W. E. Hemphill	South Carolina Press, 1959-69.
Calhoun, J. C.	*Speeches of*	*Congressional Globe*

12th Congress—Speech on War of 1812
13th Congress—Speech on incorporation of
    Bank
14th Congress—Speech on internal improve-
    ments
21st Congress—Webster-Hayne debate
22nd Congress—Speech on Force Bill
            Speech on States' Rights
24th Congress—Speech on abolition petitions
27th Congress—Speech on veto power
29th Congress—1st. Session—Speech on Oregon
  2nd. Session—Speech on Wilmot Proviso
30th Congress—Speech on Oregon
31st Congress—Speech on Slavery

Calhoun, J. C.	*Works of J. C. Calhoun,* ed. by R. K. Cralle	New York: D. Appleton, 1854.
Coit, Margaret L.	*John C. Calhoun, American Patriot*	Boston: Houghton Mifflin, 1950.
Fort Hill Address		Richmond, Virginia, 1960
Hart, Albert B.	*The American Triumverate*	New York: Mentor Assoc., 1917
Holst, Edouard von	*John C. Calhoun*	Boston: Houghton Mifflin, 1888.
Hunt, Gaillard	*John C. Calhoun*	Philadelphia: G. W. Jacobs & Co., 1907.
Meigs, William	*Life of John C. Calhoun*	New York: Neale Publishing Company, 1917.
Merriam, Charles E.	*Political Philosophy of John C. Calhoun*	New York: Studies in Southern History and Politics, 1914.
Parton, James	*Famous Americans of Recent Times*	Boston, 1867.
Pritchitt, John P.	*Calhoun, His Defense of the South*	Poughkeepsie, N.Y., 1937.
Spain, August O.	*Political Theories of John C. Calhoun*	New York: Bookman Association, 1951.
Styron, Arthur	*The Cast Iron Man*	New York: Longmans, Green, 1935.
Wiltse, Charles M.	*John C. Calhoun*	Indianapolis: Bobbs Merrill, 1944-51

INDEX

ABOUT THE AUTHOR

William D. Crane was born in New York City and attended New York schools, St. Mark's and Harvard. Graduating in February, 1916, it was his intention to make medicine his career so he went abroad armed with letters to Dr. Gros and others at the American Hospital in Neuilly, France. After a short period in the wards, he was persuaded to join the American Ambulance Field Service with whom he served six months in the field.

Returning to New York, he enrolled for pre-medical training at Columbia University, but this work was cut short by the entry of the United States into the war. He went overseas again, this time as an infantry lieutenant, and served until the end of the war. Severely gassed, medicine as a career was regretfully abandoned.

In California for his health, Mr. Crane became associated with the California Institute of Technology in Pasadena as instructor in English and Literature. After five years he resigned and opened his own school—the Crane Country Day School—where he worked until his retirement in 1945, remaining on the Board of Trustees.

He has appeared professionally in the theatre and on television. This is his fifth book for young people. He has also published a book of poems, several plays for children, a biography of Andrew Johnson and articles on education and the theatre. He and his wife live in Southport, Connecticut for part of the year, and spend their winters in Jamaica.